Jabulani!

Carol Shephard

and Bobbie Stormont

Illustrated by Kate Sheppard

Hawthorn Press

Published by Hawthorn Press, Hawthorn House, 1 Lansdown Lane, Stroud, Gloucestershire, GL5 1BJ, UK
Tel: (01453) 757040 Fax: (01453) 751138
info@hawthornpress.com
www.hawthornpress.com

Illustrations and cover illustration © Kate Sheppard
Cover design by Hawthorn Press
Design and typesetting by Lynda Smith at Hawthorn Press, Stroud, Gloucestershire
Printed in the UK by The Cromwell Press, Trowbridge, Wiltshire
CD recorded at Rookpie Recording Studios, Oldwalls, Swansea
Printed on paper sourced from sustained managed forests and elemental chlorine-free

'The Earth is Our Mother', 'Ungawa", and 'All the Earth is Sacred' from 'Circle of Song; Songs, Chants and Dances for Ritual and Celebration' compiled by Kate Marks, published by Full Circle Press © 1993 ISBN 09637489-04.
Contact information: Kate Marks/Full Circle Press, PO Box 32421, Santa Fe, NM. 87594 www.circleofsong.com
email: circle of song@earthlink.net kmarks@circleofsong.com
Extract from 'Helele Mama' reprinted by kind permission of Black Umfolosi
'Toombady', Brazilian song, written by Nana Vasconceros and arranged by Jan Hughes

Every effort has been made to trace the ownership of all copyrighted material. If any omission has been made, please bring this to the publisher's attention so that proper acknowledgment may be given in future editions.

British Library Cataloguing in Publication Data applied for

ISBN 1 903 458 51 X

Contents

Foreword

Music lifts the spirit, makes connections and creates atmosphere. Music can help people to express feelings, either in playing or in listening. Music can tell us of love and sadness, laughter and celebration. It is a universal language that can teach us about other peoples and places.

Many adults I meet have never learned an instrument and many do not have the confidence to sing. For many this is a lifelong regret – but it need not be so, and this book shows us why. It can be used by the complete beginner, but will also be useful to experienced teachers and facilitators.

Whether you are a teacher, playworker, youthworker or work with adults, parents or even very young children, you will find simple ideas for making music accessible and fun for all. No instruments? No problem. The first sections give you ideas on making your own – including finding your voice. No musical self-confidence? No worries – the practical guidance and the accompanying CD will give you all the support you need. Looking for new inspirations? The authors, Carol and Bobbie, have plenty to offer.

Whatever your age, occupation or ability, if you are working in groups the musical activities suggested here offer you a new dimension to explore and enjoy together.

Annie Davy
Head of Early Years and Childcare
Oxfordshire County Council

Acknowledgements

Bobbie would like to thank the pupils and staff of Springfield and Bardwell special schools in Oxford for providing so many opportunities for exploring and making music together; all the other schools and people attending workshops who have given so much back with their enthusiasm and new-found creativity in making music; Hilary Wainer co-founder of 'Tac Pac' and 'Beat That!' for all her experience, skill, energy and sense of fun; Dynamix Limited, Julie Latham, freelance percussionist, Pete Scott, Ali Bangoura for inspiring workshops; her friend Tracey, her family in New Zealand and Canada, and her husband Tom for their belief in her work and continued love and support.

Carol would like to thank Dynamix Limited, Play Right, Circus Eruption, Interplay and all the children and young people on play schemes for providing space and opportunity for her to learn, experiment and have fun; Beat That, Frankie Armstrong, Biddie Wells and Sarah Jewell for inspiring workshops; Scarabella for years of unrivalled singing and sharing; Sian de Lier for teaching her to make Junk Saxophones and her family, Rosa, George, Phill, Caitlin and Anna for their ever present love and support.

We both wish to thank the people of Africa with their rich tradition of chants, rhythm and harmony and their deep belief in the ability of everyone to make music; Annie Davy for the vital role she played in encouraging us to write this book; all those who have shared songs, chants and games with us over the years; Willis for his skill, sensitivity and sense of humour throughout the recording process; and all the volunteers who perform on the CD.

Before apartheid ended in South Africa in 1994 white children in white schools seldom, if ever, sang African songs and chants. But one day two young children, Casey and Kim (nieces of a friend) came home singing a chant they had learned in school that day.

That chant was Jabulani. At the time there were many more words to it than appear on the accompanying CD but the message was very clear: Jabulani, Jubilation. The black people of South Africa certainly had something to celebrate that year.

We hope this book will help you to use music to capture that kind of energy; to bring people together in a spirit of celebration.

bash bash
clunck clunck
Ding ding
bash bash.
rattle rattle
boom
boom

Introduction

If you can walk, you can dance
If you can talk, you can sing
All can and will do

Proverb from Zimbabwe

Another book on Music - Why?

Because we believe music is for everyone!
We have written this book because we want to inspire more people to make music and feel confident to lead music activities.

We want to empower people to use music. We want to give people an opportunity to challenge the belief that they can't sing, play an instrument or keep in time, and therefore that they can't lead a music session or run music activities.

We want to acknowledge that music is everyone's birthright and an integral part of being human: we are born in rhythm, we hum, we move, we dance, we rock our children: examples are apparent everywhere for everyone. We love the above proverb because it can challenge our perceptions of what we think it means to be able to sing and dance. We believe that any vocalisation or movement, however small, expressed by anyone in a music session can be part of the music making.

Music games and activities promote communication and cooperation; they build confidence and encourage participation, inclusion, creativity, spontaneity and empowerment. Even more importantly, making music is fun!

Because it is different!
This is a really practical book about how to do music that does not involve song sheets with words and music notation. Anyone will be able to make music using this book. It is user-friendly for you if you are leading a group and also for everyone joining in. We hope it is so much fun that children will pick it up, ask for an activity and maybe even lead it themselves.

It is written in our belief that everyone can participate in the activities whatever their ability, background or experience. Although we have included some suggestions for adapting activities, we encourage you to change and experiment with the games so that they remain inclusive for whoever you are making music with.

Because people have asked us!
For many years, people have been asking us to write our activities down; they ask us to put together the music games and activities they played in our workshop sessions and training so they can have a written reminder for using them in their own practice. All our

games have developed and continue to develop from our daily experience in play and education and from our own exploration of using music more freely and spontaneously.

Is this book for you?

In our experience music can change the mood of a group; it can bring a group together and can be integrated into other activities. Whether you are a playworker, teacher, childminder, youthworker, trainer or nursery nurse we want to help you feel more confident to do this with simple musical activities. These activities have been tried and tested with young children, teenagers and adults.

Everyone loves to make music and to experience being part of a band, but in our culture this is often difficult unless you have learned an instrument or feel confident about singing. In western societies music has become an elitist subject. It is often only available to the privileged few. We want to give you some tools and theory to build your confidence so that you enjoy using music and it becomes second nature. When you share this with a group they can feel empowered too. All our activities encourage leadership to be passed around and allow individuals to participate in a way that is right for them.

A special note for teachers

Music can be introduced into a classroom setting in all kinds of ways. It doesn't only have to be at times set aside for a music session. Make instruments in design and technology, play rhythm games to teach maths, explore how sounds are made in science, use song writing and chanting to promote language development (both in English and in foreign language teaching), learn about instruments from other countries and chants in different languages when you are learning geography, expand your repertoire of music and movement sessions, bring sound effects into story time. The possibilities are endless. Even tedious tasks like tidying up, queuing and getting your coats on can be made more fun with musical input: chants you all sing, using a beat to move to, call and response. There is no need to confine music making to special occasions or professional tutors; we want you to feel inspired to make music more accessible for everyone.

A word or two about inclusion

We use the word 'inclusion' a lot. It is a very important aspect of everything we do. We are committed to work in such a way that no one feels excluded by a music session. In some instances we are thinking of children who may be excluded from music-making opportunities because of sensory or physical impairments or severe and complex learning needs. However, we are also concerned with children who are shy and don't feel confident to play music; teenagers who feel they are too cool to have a go; staff who are convinced they are just not musical; and anyone at all who feels excluded by the prospect of music making in a group.

You can use the ideas in this book to run inclusive music sessions. They are tried and tested and work with anyone! However, it is our experience that whether an activity is inclusive or not is as much about the *way* you work as the activity itself. Your presentation style is the key, along with a firm belief that all those you are working with really can enjoy a music-making experience. You need to remain sensitive to people's needs and be prepared to adapt what you are doing to allow everyone to participate and to feel comfortable. The games described in this book do not have rules which must be strictly followed – use your creativity and that of your group to change and adapt them however you want.

It's also important to realise that some people experience genuine fear when faced with the prospect of playing music! You will be able to use the ideas in this book to gently draw such people in and then enjoy observing their confidence gradually build as you play more music games together.

How to use this book
This book is divided into 6 sections. The first section leads you through activities to help you 'find your instruments', making your own and exploring what you have already got. When you're ready to play them, turn to section 2 for loads of ideas on 'finding a rhythm' and making music as a band. If you'd rather sing there are activities to help you 'find your voice' in section 3.

If you want to 'find ways to bring music into other activities' then section 4 is for you. When you're ready to stop or calm down then section 5 will help you to 'find an end'.

Those who want more inspiration can 'find out more' in Bibliography, Sources and Useful Addresses.

Each activity is presented in the following way. We tell you;

- ★ What it is
- ★ What you will need
- ★ How you do it
- ★ Why we like it

You will also find:

Safety notes

These will help you to keep your music activities, instruments, environment and participants safe.

Useful tips

These tips come from our own experience in making music and playing the games in this book. They give you additional information, ideas for adapting games, and suggestions for solutions to potential difficulties.

Soundbites

These are stories that illustrate real situations from our experience in making music. They include examples of ways in which people have used, developed and adapted activities.

Drum rolls

These are bite-size chunks of theory that explain the ideas underpinning the activities. You don't have to know this stuff but it can help and you might even find it interesting.

What next?

This gives you ideas for developing the activities or suggests games you might like to play next.

A CD is included so you can hear the activities in action. You learn the songs and chants just by listening to them. This is how we work, using the age-old tradition of learning music by ear.

And last but not least...
We believe that to bring any music book or music activities alive we must instil confidence in practitioners and empower them to make and lead music. We believe everyone is musical and can take part in and lead music activities – we have proved this in our workshops and want others to be inspired by music and empowered to do likewise.

Section 1

Finding Your Instruments

Activity 1
All kinds of drums

What you will need

- ★ Tubes, e.g carpet tubes cut into sections, crisp tubes, tubs, tins such as baby milk tins
- ★ Material to stretch over the end of your tube to make a skin – rip-stop nylon works well (this is the material used to make kites), balloons are good on thin tubes, strong plastic is good too. Sharp scissors
- ★ Means to attach your skin to your drum: staple gun; thick, strong tape; big elastic bands
- ★ Decorating materials – paint, coloured paper, stickers, glue etc
- ★ Optional – something to use as a drumstick: bamboo sticks; tightly rolled and taped cardboard
- ★ Optional – ribbon or strips of material to use as carrying straps

How to do it

Take a tube and cut a piece of material so that it is at least 5 cm bigger than the end of the tube all the way round. Stretch the material tightly across the end of the tube and fix it to the sides, making sure you keep it tight all the way round. It is easier to do this bit in pairs, one person stretching, the other fixing. Once it is secure, give it a tap and see how it sounds. If the material gives way when you hit it, tighten it some more. Make a drumstick too, if you want to, or just play with the palm of your hand. Of course you can use something that doesn't need a skin, like tins for baby milk – then you just need to remove the lid, turn it upside down, decorate and make a drumstick!

Why we like it

- ★ Drums can make a big sound
- ★ They are easy to play
- ★ You can hit them with your hand or a stick so you can adapt to your own needs
- ★ Physical energy is exerted with the drumming action
- ★ Drums are great for learning rhythm games

Safety notes

If you are using carpet tubes and working with small children, cut the tube up before the session (you will need to use a small saw). You might want to use this as an opportunity to teach older children to use tools safely.

Staple guns and sharp scissors for cutting fabric also require adult supervision. Make sure you supervise children using balloons, they can easily be swallowed!

Soundbite on drums

In a mixed group of children, playworkers set up a production line where you chose your tube (or had one cut to your required size!) then went to the materials table where an adult was ready to help you to fix it with tape or staple gun. Finally you went to the decorating table to add finishing touches before everyone gathered to play their drums together!

What next?

Play some of the games in section 2 – Finding a Rhythm!

Useful tips

If you have a budget for buying musical instruments, then drums and other percussion instruments are a good investment. Over the years we have built up a collection of African drums called Djembes, along with a range of other interesting percussion instruments. All the rhythm games in section 2 work well with any kind of percussion, and a good-quality collection will last for many years and add an exciting dimension to your music making. There is a list of potential suppliers in Bibliography, Sources and Useful Addresses.

Drum roll on drums

Remember that the way drums make a sound is that the skin resonates when you hit it and the sound travels out of the open end of the drum. Children are often tempted to make a multi-purpose instrument, blocking off the other end of the tube, having filled it with bits to make a shaker. This is of course OK but it will mean that the drum will not sound so loud or clear or bright. This also applies to how you hold your drum: putting it on the floor or a table will have the same dulling effect. So you might want to make straps to hang your drum over your shoulder or around the back of your neck.

Activity 2
Shakers and other noisemakers

What you will need

★ Containers, e.g. cardboard tubes, small boxes, empty film canisters, plastic bottles, yoghurt pots, margarine tubs
★ Something to put inside the containers e.g. rice, small stones, lentils, dried peas, sand, bits of scrap card, plastic beads
★ Something to keep it all inside (card, paper, fabric, lids) held in place by tape (parcel, gaffa, masking or sellotape)
★ Decorating materials – paint, bits of fabric, ribbons, sequins, stickers, glue, tape etc.

How to do it

Choose a container. Put something in it. Cover the opening and shake it. If you like the sound it makes, cover the opening permanently by securing a lid – this might be a lid that already exists, such as from a margarine tub or film canister, or a lid you make from card, paper or fabric. Either way, secure the lid firmly with tape. Now decorate your shaker then shake, shake, shake!

If you don't like the sound your shaker makes, you can try using different fillings. Maybe you need a few more bits or maybe, as is often the case, you need less so they have more room to move around.

Why we like it

★ Shakers are easy to play
★ They make a variety of sounds
★ They can be decorated
★ You can make one very quickly or take your time!

Safety notes

Make sure your scrap is safe and clean.
Make sure you fix lids securely.
Make sure the fillings don't go into mouths or up noses.

Useful tips

Create your shakers in a space where it's OK to make a bit of a mess. Working on tables is good. Put newspaper or sheets down if working on the floor to make it easier to collect up the little bits.

What next

Once your shakers are ready, practise making a noise with them and then move on to the activities in section 2.

Soundbite on shakers

You don't need to be confined to making hand-held shakers – they can be attached with ribbons or tape to arms and legs so they rattle if you wave or stamp. You could even fix them to your body and jump and shake or tie them round your waist and wiggle African style to make a noise. Shaker hats could work too, but your neck would soon ache! On one playscheme we securely attached little shakers to wheelchair wheels so as the wheels went round the shakers would make a noise.

Drum roll on scrap materials

Collecting household scrap is a great free resource and good for recycling. However, be sure that any containers are empty and clean with no splits or sharp edges. Be especially wary of containers which held milk products. It is also recommended that for reasons of hygiene you do not recycle toilet roll tubes.

As for shaker fillers, avoid dried kidney beans as they are poisonous if eaten raw. Also be aware that small children might put objects like beads or peas in their mouths or up their noses.

You can also buy scrap materials cheaply from a scrap store – check with your local play association or council to find one near to you.

Activity 3
Junk saxophones and other windy things

What you will need

- ★ Straws
- ★ Glass bottles
- ★ Plastic pots (the kind used for large yoghurts or small ice creams!)
- ★ Cardboard, plastic or rubber tubing
- ★ Balloons
- ★ Card
- ★ Scissors, a sharp knife, a sharp point like a bradawl or a drill, tape, decorating materials

How to do it

You can start by experimenting with how a reed works in a wind instrument by taking a straw, flattening the end and cutting two triangle shapes off the top so you are left with a point. Place the point in your mouth and blow. You may need to adjust the pressure you place on the straw with your lips – experiment until you make a surprisingly loud sound! You can then try making holes in the straw and covering them up as if you were playing a recorder and see if you can change the note you produce.

Try blowing across the top of a glass bottle and hear the sound resonate. Different bottles make different sounds. You will need to change the shape of your mouth and blow across your bottom lip, pressed to the edge of the top of the bottle. This is similar to the technique used when playing a flute.

A junk saxophone can be made using an empty plastic pot (the kind you buy yoghurt and ice cream in) a length of cardboard, plastic or rubber tubing and a balloon. Make a hole in the bottom of the pot, just big enough to poke the tube through. Now make a hole in the side of the pot, about halfway down. Cut the neck off the balloon and stretch the rest across the top of the plastic pot. Secure the balloon in place with some tape. Ensure the end of the tube touches the balloon and the rest pokes out from the bottom of the pot. Secure the tube in place with tape – it must be airtight. Now your 'saxophone' is ready to play. Just blow into the hole in the side of the pot. This will make the balloon resonate, and the sound will come out of the tube. It can take a little subtlety to play a junk saxophone so persevere with your blowing technique if there is no sound at first! Try adjusting the position of the tube. You can also experiment with cutting holes in the tube and covering them with your fingers to change the sound; or fixing a short tube into the side hole so you have a 'mouthpiece' to blow into.

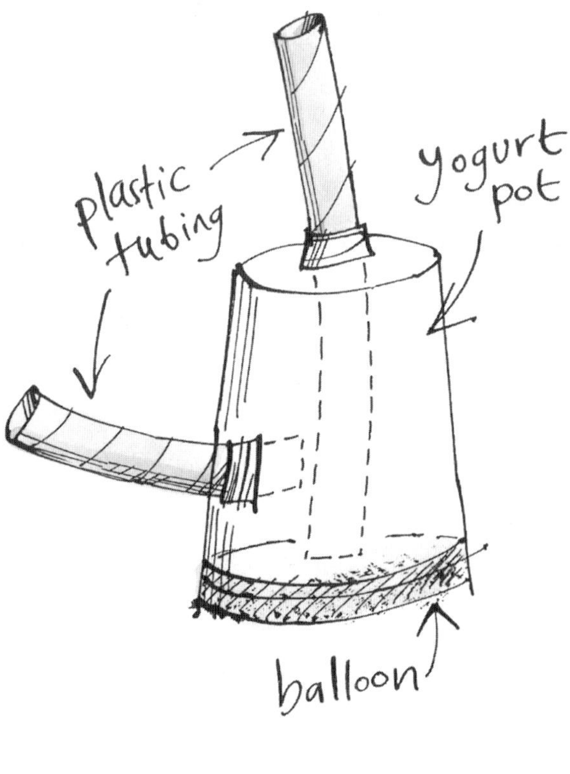

Didgeridoos are another possibility but also require a certain degree of skill to learn the playing technique. All you need is a long tube, the end of which will fit over your mouth. Place your lips together and blow, keeping the lips and face relaxed. Without the didgeridoo in place you make a sound like a horse! You will need to experiment in order to get a sound that is sonorous rather than rude!

If you prefer to keep things simpler you can make trumpets from semi-circles of card, rolled into a cone shape, secured with tape and decorated. Sing toot, toot or doo, doo onto your cone and enjoy how your voice is amplified as you play your trumpet!

Why we like it

- ★ Wind instruments can add a new dimension to your music making
- ★ It makes a change from percussion
- ★ The sounds you make are often very funny
- ★ It takes a little patience and experimentation to make a sound
- ★ Someone who finds it hard to bang a drum or shake a shaker in time might enjoy blowing instead

Safety notes

Take particular care when leading activities which require the use of scissors, sharp knives, drills or bradawls. We usually allocate the cutting and hole-making to one supervising adult who is responsible for the equipment throughout the session.

Soundbite on wind instruments

Due to the quite rude sound you can make when blowing a straw, some children who were dismissive of joining in with our music-making suddenly found it more appealing!

Soundbite on junk saxophones

At an environment festival children attended a workshop to make themselves a junk saxophone and learn how to play it. There was a wonderful array of different tones which sounded spectacular when they blew the rhythm of a song together for the closing parade.

Useful tip

Another handy 'windy thing' is a whistle, particularly if you are going to create a carnival (see section 4, activity 6). However, lots of whistles can be overwhelming!

What next?

If you manage to get a good sound from your didgeridoo, try playing it with the end resting on a resonance board (see section 1, activity 6). The sensation for the person lying on the board is wonderful and relaxing.

Drumroll on wind instruments

Instruments you blow are called wind instruments and sound is made by creating a vibrating column of air inside the tube of the instrument. Whether it is a straw, a piece of curled metal tubing in a brass instrument or a wooden recorder, the tube forms a container for a column of air and the vibrations of this column of air produce the sounds we hear. You can change the sound, or pitch of the note you play by increasing or decreasing the length of the tube or by opening and closing holes along the tube to control where air enters and exits. You can experiment with this by playing a straw, as described above, and then gradually cutting bits off the bottom – the note you play will get higher as the straw gets shorter.

When you have a reed, the sound is made when the frequency of vibration of the reed matches the frequency of vibration of the air column in the tube. This is why you have to experiment a bit when you blow into your straw – you are naturally searching for the right frequency.

Activity 4
What have you got already? Discovering instruments in your environment

What you will need

* Confidence to explore the sounds you can make with your own body
* Willingness to use your imagination to try making sounds with objects around you
* A few sticks, some with softened ends, can be useful
* Some agreed ground rules about respecting the environment
* Optional – some props to experiment with (see below)

How to do it

Start with your own bodies and explore the different sounds you can make. Begin with obvious things like clapping your hands and stamping your feet. Try patting your thighs and tapping them with your fingertips. Remember the sounds can be subtle! You can tap your teeth, your knuckles and your fingernails, even hold a strand of hair on your head and pluck it like a double bass string! If you open your mouth wide by dropping your jaw, your stretched cheeks will resonate when tapped. Changing the shape of your mouth will change the tone of the sound you make. Some children (and adults too!) will delight in producing windy sounds by cupping their hands in their armpits and squeezing. If this is the case you can expand on this with straws – place one end of a straw into your closed armpit and the other end in your mouth: blow and delight in the unpleasant sounds you can create!

Having explored your own bodies, you can widen your attention to the environment you are in. This is where you need to agree ground rules about respecting the environment, then start tapping and hitting things to see what sounds they make. Indoors you will find that radiators make a lovely sound when hit with a softened stick, metal chair legs often resonate when hit, as does a table top if you hit it with the palm of your hand, or tap it with your finger tips. Closed doors, especially those with a cupboard behind them, will boom when struck with the palm of your hand; or simply knock. If you are outside, find sticks and hit them together, strike metal railings, hit drain covers, pick up a handful of small stones, cup your hands and shake them. The key to this activity is to keep trying out different ideas.

If you want to introduce other things to experiment with, bring in bunches of keys, coins, plastic bags to rustle between your hands and then clap, or sweep with brooms. You can get inspiration for this kind of music making from the internationally famous group 'Stomp'.

After a period of experimenting get everyone to choose their instrument and then play the games in section 2!

Why we like it

- ★ You don't need to have expensive instruments
- ★ You don't need to make a mess making instruments
- ★ You start with nothing except yourselves and can still create exciting music
- ★ The exploration is fun
- ★ You can pitch the activity according to your group
- ★ You can start playing when you are out and about

Safety notes

Some people may be horrified that we are advocating hitting furniture; but with clearly defined boundaries and a bit of common sense, children hitting a chair leg with a stick or slapping a tabletop with their hands are unlikely to cause any damage. Agreeing not to hit glass is sensible, although a line of milk bottles with differing amounts of water in them makes a fabulous xylophone when hit with a stick! As with any activity, use your own judgement with your own group.

Useful tip

If you want to make a soft drumstick, wrap cotton wool or soft fabric around the end of the stick and fix it in place with strong tape. Chopsticks make a nice sound too. If you want to do some preparation before the session, you can introduce objects like old saucepans, plastic bins, metal hubcaps and plastic piping (hit the end with the sole of a shoe or better still, a flip-flop!).

Soundbite on using your environment

A group of lively teenagers who were not at all interested in making their own instruments really got into this activity and played a wonderful and fairly challenging combination of rhythms with the basic beat kept by a lad playing the cupboard door, a section of drummers slapping tables, another section of 'metallic sounds' (chair legs, door handles, keys) responding to their rhythm and a vocal section making a range of spontaneous whoops, whistles and calls over the top of it all!

Activity 5
Air guitars and other figments of the imagination

What you will need

- ★ Materials such as large sheets of cardboard, boxes, tubes, empty plastic containers, fabric, paper
- ★ Equipment to fix and decorate: scissors, tape, string, stapler, glue, paint, pens etc
- ★ Space to make a mess or cover the floor
- ★ A safe space to let the imagination flow!

How to do it

Get your group to make instruments from the materials, which they can play by miming or providing the sounds themselves. For example, cut out electric guitar shapes from large sheets of cardboard, make straps, draw on some strings, decorate and play! Either sing the guitar part or mime to a prerecorded piece of music. Don't stop at guitars: make saxophones, trumpets, flutes, keyboards ... see where the imagination of your group takes you!

Why we like it

- ★ It can draw in children who are less keen to play real instruments
- ★ You can develop other performance skills like singing, dancing and mime
- ★ It can look very effective if a 'band' forms and performs
- ★ It is great fun!

Soundbite on air guitars and other figments of the imagination

A lot of the girls on a playscheme were devising dance routines and miming to current chart hits, practising to perform for the other children. A group of three older boys, who were unimpressed to the point of becoming disruptive, were captivated by the playworkers' suggestion to make cool electric guitars

and be a 'real' band, playing 'real' music. They threw themselves into the task and before long were making themselves wigs of long hair and planning what to wear, and whose CD they were going to mime to. They became one of the most memorable acts of the summer!

Drum roll on performance

Performing in front of your peers can be a daunting experience for many children and young people. It is our belief that first and foremost the kinds of music activity we are promoting are about the process and not any end result. We want people to enjoy the experience of making music and not feel any additional extra pressure to perform. However, it is often the case that as an activity develops it reaches a point where the participants feel they want an audience and a chance to show off the fruits of their efforts. When this happens it is an opportunity for you to take things further, maybe using some of the ideas in section 4. Take it slowly though, and remain sensitive. If you have managed to coax someone from the shadows, do not be tempted to lead him[1] straight into the limelight!

Activity 6
Resonance boards

An unusual drum which enables you to feel the beat, rhythm and music through your whole body.

What you will need

- ★ Wood – 5cm x 2.5cm (2" x 1") enough to make a frame to measure 150cm x 110cm (5' x 3' 8")
- ★ Plywood – 4mm or 5mm thick. This usually comes in a sheet 240cm x 120cm (8' x 4')
- ★ Wood glue
- ★ Screwdriver and wood screws
- ★ Sandpaper
- ★ Varnish
- ★ Paint (optional for decorating)

How to do it

Make a frame from the 5cm x 2.5cm (2" x 1") wood to measure 150cm x 110cm (5' x 3' 8"). Sand off any rough edges or corners. The plywood usually comes in a sheet 240cm x 120cm (8' by 4'). It is absolutely fine to make your resonance board measure 120cm x 120cm (4' x 4') thus getting two boards out of one sheet of ply. We suggest 150cm (5') in length so adults can lie comfortably on it and we suggest 110cm (3' 8") in width because this gives us maximum width to still fit the board into the back of an estate car.

Once your frame is made, cut your plywood to the required length and

[1] To avoid the awkward use of both genders, we will alternate from section to section

width, and glue it and screw it securely onto the frame. Sand down the plywood making sure there are no rough edges. If you want to decorate your board this is the time to do so. Then apply two or three coats of varnish according to the maker's instructions. The smaller sheet of plywood left over could become another resonance board for young children. You are now ready to learn to play your new and unusual instrument!

Why we like it

- ★ A group can work together to make a resonance board
- ★ It can be decorated
- ★ You can play it like a big drum with hands or beaters
- ★ You can use it on the floor or a table
- ★ You can feel the basic beat, rhythm and sound through your whole body – a bit like a body massage
- ★ People who find it difficult to hold instruments can participate in and lead music making.

Safety notes

Make your resonance board where there is ample space, light and air.
Make it where it is OK to make a bit of a mess.
Make sure there is someone with you who is very experienced and confident with using tools.
Make sure you sand down any rough edges or surfaces on your board.

Useful tips

If you use the board on the floor make sure the space is big enough for the board and space round the outside of the board for up to 8 people to sit on the floor.

Make it comfy for the players by putting mats or cushions around the outside of the board for people to sit on.

If you use the board on a table or two tables pushed together make sure the board fits the table and doesn't hang over the sides as you will lose the resonance if the surface of the plywood board touches the table top.

What next?

Once your resonance board is ready, have a go at making drumming sounds on the board with your fingers. Use it like a big drum. Before anyone lies on the board read activity 2 in section 2. Introduce people to the board slowly. The sound level in Rumbles can be very high, so be very careful if you have people in your group who are sound-sensitive. They may like to sit on the mat round the outside of the board and just put their feet on it, or lie on the board with a pillow under their heads. Don't drum too loudly too soon. Listen to what those lying on the board say – 'Not so loud!' or 'I want it loud but not by my head'. For those who cannot communicate this with words make sure you know how they can let you know they do not like something, and listen to them.

Now you are ready to move onto other rhythm activities in section 2.

Soundbite on resonance boards

We use resonance boards with everyone, but particularly with children and young people who have learning difficulties and complex needs or who are physically disabled. Sometimes they lie on the board or put their feet or hands on the board while we make rhythm patterns round the outside. Often, for the first time, they 'feel' sound through their whole bodies. Through the rhythms and music we play on the board they become more aware of where their feet are or even their shoulders, fingertips, back of their heads etc. Music-making on the board encourages them to participate with their voices and bodies, learning to conduct and shape the music.

In a class I once taught there were two young lads with physical and learning disabilities. It was very difficult for them to have eye contact and physical contact with others. One day we got them to lie down on the board together in such a way that if they rolled onto their side or turned their heads they might make eye contact – and possibly physical contact – with each other. This is exactly what happened. Their eyes and hands met. It was such a lovely social occasion for them, which developed through music-making on the resonance board.

We have also discovered that everyone wants to have a go and enjoy feeling sound and rhythm through their bodies. We all want to experience a sound massage and be immersed in music-making, so don't forget to allow everyone to have a go and talk about how it feels.

Drum roll on the resonance board

The resonance board was originally designed by Lilli Nielsen. She describes its purpose as follows:

> The resonance-platform reinforces every sound the infant or child makes with every movement of his body, by pushing or any other activity with toys around him. The aim of the resonance-platform was to give blind infants and children auditory feedback of their activities.[2]

In practice in special schools the boards were used in two ways: children with visual or hearing impairments lay on the board with toys and objects around them and as described above they would receive auditory feedback when they accidentally pushed, hit or banged one of the toys or objects. It was hoped that gradually these children would intentionally pick up the objects or push them, thus laying important foundations for future communication and also giving them some control over their environment. Physiotherapists and occupational therapists also began to use them when they worked with children on their exercises, making the experience more enjoyable. In latter years people have begun to use them as we have, as a musical instrument and a great big drum. Resonance boards have brought a new dimension to music-making for children and young people with complex needs, enabling them to experience and participate in creating music and more fully enjoy the social dimension of music.

[2] Nielsen, 1988, p35

Section 2

Finding a Rhythm

Activity 1
The stop-start game

CD track 1

Ideas for organising exuberant music makers or ... How to control the chaos!

What you will need

- ★ Percussion instruments, ones you have made or bought. Don't forget your body as a percussion instrument
- ★ Drums
- ★ Space to sit in a circle

How to do it

When you want to create a space or silence in the music-making or stop it altogether this is what you do:

Stopping

Using a big, strong, voice call a ... a ... a ... and STOP! The 'and' happens over 4 beats, as follows:

a......... a......... a......... and STOP!

1 2 3 4 STOP!

As you call, use your body too so people know something is going to happen e.g. begin lifting your arms. Finally on the STOP lift your arms right up in the air so everyone has no doubt that the music-making is to STOP! Encourage everyone to lift their arms up – if they are in the air they are not playing instruments!

What follows naturally is a silence. You can enjoy this silence before starting your music-making again or you can choose this to be the end of your music-making.

Starting

If you are using percussion with young children it is helpful to exaggerate the starting bit of your playing by including 'playful' anticipation. By doing this they quickly experience the pleasure of starting to make music all together.

The starting signal needs to be big and bold, so make sure all eyes are on you. Begin with your arms up in the air and, moving your fingers, ask everyone to copy you. Then slowly bring your arms down. Say something like ' Slowly bring your arms down, like the rain falling, slowly, slowly, not too fast'. Tease this out. When everyone's hands are just above their drum or near their instrument take in a big 'noisy breath', lifting your arms up again just a little. Pause for 1 or 2 seconds, building anticipation and gaining eye contact. Then as you let your breath out, bring your hands onto your drum or pick up your instrument and begin your music-making again.

A good activity for practising the start-stop game is activity 2 in this section.

Why we like it

- ★ We can allow children to make very loud sounds and music especially on drums and know we can control it
- ★ Everyone can be a leader, calling the stop and controlling the start
- ★ It can be easily adapted to individual abilities and skills
- ★ It is a superb way to gain everyone's attention at any time
- ★ You experience that silences in music are just as important as the music-making itself
- ★ It builds anticipation

Soundbite on the 'Stop-start game'

Children just love this game and ask to play it again and again, especially when linked with activity 2 in this section, 'Rumbles'. It is not long before even very young children are calling the stop appropriately. Sometimes in the silence after a stop we have used the space to say what we are going to do next in the music-making, without detracting from the music itself, and then we can start again.

We had one little boy during a music session who had not managed to be part of the group at all, and just as we finished he came over to the board and led us in a drumming game, stopping and starting us three times and then saying 'That's all!' He was truly empowered.

Useful tips

- ★ If you are working with children or young people who might find it difficult to call out the word stop, they could hold up a stop sign or use a switch on a tape-player, on which you have previously recorded the a… a… a… and STOP!
- ★ Experiment with your voice, making it go up as you say a… a…a…and STOP! Those who can't raise their arms may be able to join in or lead with their voices
- ★ It also helps as you lift your arms right up and call STOP to lift one knee high and give a good stamp on the floor at the same time
- ★ Once you have stopped, maintain the silence, don't rush to begin again too soon
- ★ Try using the space you created after the Stop for individuals to play their particular instrument or for a group to play instruments that make a particular sound, e.g. wooden instruments, or shakers, or air guitars etc.
- ★ For older groups try counting to 4 to bring them in again. Make sure everyone is watching you, then count 1 2 3 4, lifting your arms up on the count of 3 and bringing them down on the count of 4 as a sign for people to play their instrument again.

What next?

Try the Stop-start game with the next activity in this section, 'Rumbles'.

You can find your own ways of stopping and starting. You might agree on a particular drum rhythm. People will have to listen very carefully to hear the rhythm that tells them to stop or start. Try some activities in this section and build in a stop and start.

Drum roll on stopping and starting

Everything we do has a beginning and an ending. We are usually in charge of that ourselves. When a group needs some organisation or is engaged in an activity together it becomes really important for everyone to know how things will begin and end and what the signal is if we all need to stop and listen to something important.

This becomes even more important in music-making, especially when there are lots of percussion instruments and drums – such exciting instruments to play: everything is getting a bit chaotic, everyone wants to play at once, the noise level is getting high, and it is time to stop and refocus the music-making in some way.

Activity 2
Rumbles

CD track 1

A game to enjoy playing your percussion instruments, quietly and very loudly, playing as a band, practising stopping and starting and 'creating a fruitful silence'.

What you will need

★ Anything to make a noise with, percussion instruments, drums, or your body
★ Space to sit or stand in a circle

How to do it

Begin the 'rumble' by playing your instruments very, very, very, quietly. If you have drums just play them with your fingertips. After you have rumbled for a bit, conduct the band so they get a little bit louder. Simply say 'a little bit louder'. Rumble at this level for a bit and then again conduct the band to get a bit louder. As you get louder, those drumming with fingers will need to change to using their whole hand. You might notice people beginning to smile – they can't believe they are allowed to play louder and louder. Keep going until the rumbling is very loud. It will naturally be getting faster and faster too, so go with it, and play loud and fast.

When you are ready, call a stop (see activity 1 in this section). Exaggerate the a...a...a...and with your mouth so people see and hear that the Stop is coming. A... a... a... and... STOP!

When this game is new for people, once the rumbles have stopped they usually laugh or giggle or express their excitement and pleasure in some way.

Just let this happen, but before the excitement is lost begin rumbling all over again.

Why we like it

- ★ You can use any surface inside or out to drum on
- ★ You can use your bodies, e.g. hands drumming on knees
- ★ It gives permission for people to play loud and fast
- ★ It creates a magical silence at the end
- ★ It makes people smile
- ★ It uses lots of energy
- ★ It helps get rid of tension
- ★ It's very exciting

Safety notes

The sound level in rumbling can be very high, so be very careful if you have people in your group who are sound-sensitive. You may have to build it very slowly for them; they may dislike the very loud sounds altogether and may need to move away from the group for a bit. Some percussion instruments, e.g. seedpods on a stick, can be very loud and actually hurt the ears, so choose the percussion for this activity carefully.

The loud rumbles on the resonance board can also be too much for some people, so check it out with those lying on the board. For those who cannot communicate this with words make sure you know how they can let you know they do not like something, and listen to them.

What next?

Once you have played the game several times, encourage people to maintain the silence that naturally follows after you call the Stop. It helps to keep your arms up in the air to give a visual clue that the Stop is still going on. This can then become a fruitful silence into which children with profound and complex needs can vocalise or move, especially if you have made the rumbles on a resonance board with them lying on the board.

You may like to use the silence as a space to listen to particular instruments or vocal sounds.

Try stopping the rumbles when they are not very loud, leaving a silence and starting the rumbles again quietly, and building them up again.

Try conducting the rumbles to make them get louder and softer (see activity 15 in this section, 'Orchestration') and shaping the rumble before you let rip and go for the 'full monty!'

Try the rumbles as a 'pile up' either round the group or randomly (see activity 14 in this section).

Soundbite on rumbles

We have found rumbles to be fantastic when used on resonance boards. People have told us it is the best all over massage they have had in ages and it leaves their fingers and toes tingling.

For children and young people with profound and complex needs it is one of the best ways to feel all their body all at once; or specific body parts if rumbling, for example, just round the hands and fingers or just round a shoulder. The huge contrast between the loudness of the rumble, the Stop and the ensuing silence really wakes up their ears. Being able to hear and differentiate sounds is paramount for the development of language. Children with such specific needs have responded in the silence with gorgeous vocalisations; and everybody heard them, they had a place of honour in the silence. Yipee!

A group of adults played 'rumbles' on drums and at the end one woman laughed and said 'I felt as if I was doing something really naughty, it was fabulous'.

Drum roll on creating a fruitful silence

We are surrounded by a great mix of noise and sounds during the day, some of them organised and some of them random, some pleasant, familiar and comforting and some that annoy us, are unpleasant and even hurt our ears. The environment can be very busy with sound and hard on our ears and our wellbeing. It can be quite chaotic.

It is therefore very important to create some silence and space to rest our ears and let them begin to tune into individual sounds, differentiate sounds and begin to understand that music is as much about silences as it is about sound. Our ears never have to work so hard as when there is silence. Try it.

You know how amazing it is to go outside at night, look up and see the stars in the sky or turn off all the lights in the house to light the candles on a birthday cake. When we do this we are cutting out other visual distractions so our eyes are better able to focus on one thing. It is not so easy to do this for our ears, but creating a fruitful silence is one such way.

It is therefore good to create silences in music sessions, or, once there is silence, to offer it as a space for people to fill with their voice, instrument or movement. In this way a silence becomes a fruitful silence and it can be as long as you like. You will be able to judge this because you know your group. Silences can be especially important for people in your group who have learning difficulties or specific needs, e.g. a visual or hearing impairment, a difficulty concentrating, an inability to hold instruments or use them independently, and those who take time to respond.

In music we can make fruitful silences by creating huge contrasts between the presence of sound and the absence of sound or by building our music to a crescendo and then stopping it.

If you have had quite a lot of experience making music with a group or listening to music, you will notice that the spaces and silences can be quite short, but it is what happens in the spaces that livens up the music and gives it that 'swing' that makes you want to click your fingers, tap your toes and get up and dance.

Activity 3
The basic beat

CD tracks 2, 3 and 4

Two activities to help us

- ★ feel the basic beat in our bodies
- ★ know its importance in making music
- ★ hold the basic beat for any music we create

What you will need

- ★ CD player and your favourite CDs
- ★ Space to move around

1. Feeling that beat

How to do it

Put on favourite CDs and tracks that have a strong backing drumbeat and simply move to them. Whether you move your feet, click your fingers or sway your body you will be moving to the basic beat.

Try counting the basic beat 1 2 3 4 as you move.

Try beating a drum, keeping in time with the beat on the CD track.

Dance and enjoy.

Why we like it

- ★ Everyone gets a chance to share their favourite tracks
- ★ You feel the basic beat straight away and begin to know how important it is as the foundation of all music-making
- ★ People naturally begin adding finger clicks or body movements and jazzing things up. You can use this natural talent later to liven up your own music-making

Useful tip

If you see some people struggling to move in time with the music, try walking round the room to the beat of the music or doing simple actions for everyone to copy.

What next?

Play more games in section 2 and make up some of your own.

2. Legging it

What you will need

Everyone standing in a circle

How to do it

You are going to 'walk' the basic beat on the spot, feeling it through your legs and feet firmly into the floor. You are just emphasising what you do naturally when you get up on the dance floor and move to music.

Begin to move by stepping your right foot to the right and bringing your left foot in beside it. Then move your left foot to the left and step your right foot in beside it. Putting this to our 4 beats it will look like this:

1
step right & bring in left foot
2
step left & bring in right foot
3
step right & bring in left foot
4
step left & bring in right foot

Ask everyone to copy you.

Useful tips

Some people will be opposite you in the circle and so will begin on their left foot. As a result some people will be bumping hips with the person next to them. This is OK and actually gets people laughing and relaxing. Let it happen and then remind people how hard it is to copy when you are facing the leader and how difficult it might be for others when we say 'Copy me'. The group will find their own way round this eventually, but if they do need a clue, try saying this at the same time:

1		2		3		4	
'Right	&	left	&	right	&	left' ...	I said
'Right	&	left	&	right	&	left'	

Step to the right on the first beat and on the '&' bring the left foot in beside it. Step to the left on beat 2 and on the '&' bring the right foot in beside it, etc.

What next?

Once people are moving more freely, keep this basic beat in your feet going and try saying the following rap over the top...

Feel it in your feet
It's the basic beat
mm- aah- mm mm- ah
Right & left & right & left
Fingers tap it in the car
Feet stamp it at the bar
It's the basic beat, feel it in your feet
Mm- aah- mm mm- ah
Without this beat, music there is not
It's just sound and noise – so give it
all you've got
Right & left & right & left

Feel it in your feet
It's the basic beat
Mm- aah- mm mm- ah

A... a... a... and STOP –

What next?

Keeping the beat going in your feet and putting another layer of music on top.

- ★ Clap a rhythm and get everyone to clap it back. Repeat this several times
- ★ Make a call as in Repeat after me section 3 activity 3, CD track 19
- ★ Make up any other body percussion or actions for people to copy
- ★ Pass the leadership around and encourage others to make a clap, call, or movement

When you've had enough, call the STOP: a... a... a... and STOP!

Useful tip

If people are struggling with keeping the basic beat in their feet and putting another layer on top, try the claps and calls without your feet and then try them together. It's a bit like patting your head and rubbing your tummy in a circle at the same time.

Drum roll on the basic beat

In music we are surrounded by rhythms. Within these rhythms there is a regular pulse which sets our toes a-tapping or our bodies rocking. This pulse develops by grouping beats e.g.

1 2 3 4 1 2 3 4........
(4 time – as in a march)

or

1 2 3 1 2 3 1 2 3......
(3 time – as in a waltz or rocking lullaby)

We call this the basic beat. This basic beat is the foundation of any music we make. We may not always hear it but we certainly feel it! We begin to keep time to the music and tune into the basic beat.

Imagine a brick wall with a solid foundation. This foundation supports all the other layers of bricks that will go on top. If the foundation is strong we can make changes in the layers, perhaps miss a brick here and there, make a gap, create a pattern. In music the basic beat is the foundation of our wall of sound. Once that is strong and in place, we can build layers of sound and rhythm on top. If at any time the layers begin to 'shake' or the music falls apart and chaos seems to reign, no problem! The foundation will still be there. The basic beat remains. Everyone can return to playing the basic beat and we can begin again building layers and creating a new wall of rhythm.

Activity 4
One, two, who are you?

CD track 5

A game to get to know people's first and family names

What you will need

- ★ Everyone in a circle sitting or standing
- ★ A drum

How to do it

Begin by beating 2 strong and steady beats on your drum and at the same time calling out the 2 beats. It looks like this:

Play on drum	1	2
& call out	one	two

After the 1 2 beat, call out the first and family name of the first person in the circle in the same time as the strong 1 2 beat. It will now look like this:

Play on drum	1	2
& call out	one	two
Play on drum	1	2
& call out	Mark	Williams

Once people know the game and feel confident you can let people say their own names after the 1 2 beat and call.

It's a game that keeps the basic beat moving and gets better the more you play it.

Why we like it

- ★ You can adapt the game easily so everyone can take part
- ★ Each person is celebrated by name
- ★ People's family names are heard, often for the first time
- ★ You can vary the pace depending on the group you are playing it with
- ★ You can find out other things about each other – favourite food, pop groups etc.
- ★ It's a good game to learn simple signing for people's names, favourite foods etc.

Soundbite on One, two, who are you?

When we tried out this game on a group of young children with language delay some children couldn't say their family name. One of the teaching assistants came up with a great idea. After the beat and call, a child who couldn't say the family name just said her first name, and the rest of the group who could, called out their family name. Some children were unable to say their names at all, but were able to beat the 1 2 on a drum. They therefore took it in turns to be the leader, beating out the 1 2 each time, and were supported in this if they needed it. It soon became obvious that this was a very important role to have and all the children were keen to be the leader.

What next?

Try leaving out the call 1 2 and just beating it on the drum. Try beating it quietly and have people say their name using the same quieter dynamic.

Have fun by encouraging people to say their names in different ways, e.g. high, low.

Get people to make a body shape for their first name and another body shape for their second name. So after you have made the 1 2 call on the drum, each person responds in turn with body shapes rather than saying their names.

Try putting other things in after the 1 2 call, e.g. all the countries in Africa, foods you like, pets, pop groups etc., or even the sound of one of the instruments you made in section 1.

Activity 5
Vanessa's game

CD tracks 6 and 7

A game to feel and move to the basic beat, both the marching beat and the lullaby beat. A game to use and feel spaces, to leave them or fill them.

What you will need

★ Space to sit in a circle

How to do it

1. Playing Vanessa's game to a marching 4-beat rhythm

You are going to walk round the outside of the circle, lightly touching people on their shoulders. As you touch someone's shoulders the rest of the group calls out that person's first name. Then you move to the next person, touch her shoulders and the others call out her name. You will build up a rhythm as you go - 1 2 3 4. Each person is 1 beat. Start slowly and steadily. It would look like this.

1	2	3	4
Gillian	Rashid	David	Robert

As the 4-beat rhythm emerges people can beat it on their knees. Continue round the group until you are back at the beginning.

See what it sounds and feels like if everyone calls softly or loudly or one name soft and then one loud. You can decide how you will call before you begin. You will soon know if you need to move more slowly or more quickly round the group.

What next?

Begin to walk round as before, but when you get to the 4th person don't touch her shoulders or call her name, simply stand behind her and call STOP. In other words you are leaving a space on beat number 4. It helps if everyone calls out STOP on that beat while they get used to a space being there instead of someone's name. At the same time as they call STOP on beat 4, raise your arms high up in the air, palms forward and fingers stretched making a visual STOP.

Once they are used to this space, leave it as a space and listen to the silence. Do this several times.

As we all know, if there is ever a space anywhere, in our cupboards or in the car park, we like to fill it. This is a lovely opportunity for you to fill the space with a simple movement, e.g. legs out and arms up like a star or standing on one leg, or bob down and come back up, or a jump etc.

2. Playing Vanessa's game to a swing or 3-beat rhythm

This time we use the beat of the lullaby, the swing and the waltz – a 3-beat rhythm:

1 2 3   1 2 3   1 2 3   1 2 3

If you say this aloud it will begin to take on a lilting quality and you can imagine a swing going back and forwards.

You walk round the outside of the group as before but this time as the group calls the names, they also call out 'and' in between each one. This will change the feel of the beat and the way in which you walk round the outside. You touch someone's shoulder and she calls the name, then when the group says 'and' you have a little pause or breath as you move to the next person. The game and calling becomes much softer.

It looks like this:

1 2 3 1 2 3 1 2 3
Mary **and** Abdhul **and** Vanessa **and**

1 2 3
Tom **and** etc right round the group.

Once you get the swing of the three beats you'll find you can dance your way around with a skip or a turn on the 'and' in between each person's name!

What next?

Begin to walk round as before. You are still going to make your STOP when you get to the 4th person. As before, don't touch her shoulder or call her name, simply stand behind her and call STOP. It helps if everyone calls out STOP on that beat while they get used to a space being there instead of someone's name. At the same time that they call STOP, raise your arms high up in the air, palms forward and fingers stretched making a visual STOP.

Once they are used to this space, leave it as a space and listen to the silence. Do this several times. As before, you can leave it as a space or fill it with a statue-like pose or even a lovely dance twirl. The 3-beat rhythm lends itself to this very well.

Why we like it

- ★ Because Vanessa, who was only 9, made it up
- ★ It is especially good if you have someone new in your group and they don't know many people's names

- ★ You feel the 2 types of beat very strongly in your body
- ★ You begin to hear silences in music and learn how to use them
- ★ People become very creative in the spaces with movements and percussion
- ★ It is a hot favourite with groups

Useful tip

It is always good to check first that people don't mind being touched lightly on their shoulders.

If some people are finding it difficult to move with the beat you can buddy them and move round with them until they get the idea. If some people find physically moving from one place to another difficult, then the 3-beat swing rhythm is great because it doesn't matter how long you say the 'and' for – you just keep on saying it until 'Vanessa' reaches the next person and touches her shoulder. So it might look like this:

1 2 3 1 2 3
Mary **and** Abdhul **a.........nd**

1 2 3 1 2 3
Vanessa **a.......and** Tom **and**

What next?

Once you have played around and lots of people have had a turn at being 'Vanessa', try leaving the space on another beat, maybe beat 3, then beat 2 and even beat 1.

What happens if you leave a space on beat 2 and beat 4?

What if you put a click or two or three in the space? Or play some percussion?

You will begin to experience what it is that gives music 'swing', that aliveness that has you clicking your fingers and stamping your feet.

Soundbite on Vanessa's game

We were working in an inclusive primary school where the local special school had 3 classes of children on a permanent basis. The groups we had for music sessions were always mixed. Some children were finding it very difficult to keep the basic beat so we began to go round calling children's names every time we beat a drum. I thought we needed to include movement somehow and said so, without knowing quite what we might do. Vanessa got up and began to go round the outside of the circle touching the children as we called the names. It soon became apparent that we didn't need to concentrate on beating on the drum, since everyone could see the beat happening as Vanessa touched shoulders, and they could hear it happening as they called a name.

As Vanessa was going round she began to dance it with flowing arms and 'ballet'-like turns, changing the marching 4 beat quite naturally into the flowing 3 beat. Quite amazing.

Moving the beat in this way really helped some children enormously, especially when they had a go at being 'Vanessa'.

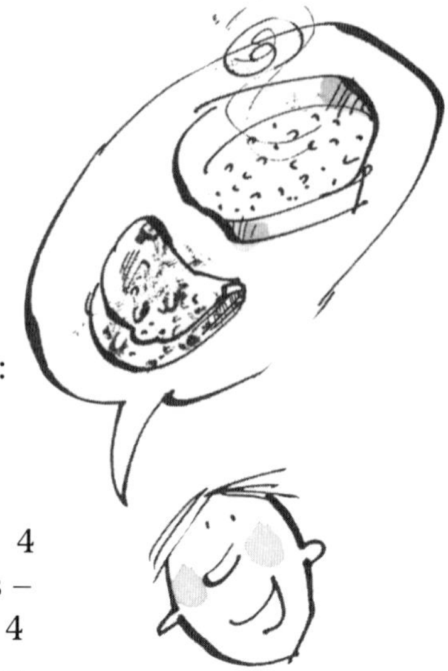

Activity 6
Foodies

CD track 8

A game to make your mouth water

What you will need

- ★ Something to drum on
- ★ Everyone sitting in a circle

How to do it

Play a strong, steady beat – 1 2 3 4 – on table tops, drums, resonance boards, wheelchair, trays etc. This is the first step, the foundation of the wall. It is like a march. Keep it going continually. This solid beat gives us a feeling of strength, energy and togetherness. We can now put another layer of our sound wall on top.

Everyone keeps the basic beat going, but when you are ready for the 'Foodies', conduct for people to play more quietly in order to hear the next layer. One at a time, go round the group and say what you like to drink or eat, e.g.: fish and chips, sausage and beans, chappati and dahl, spaghetti bolognaise, poppadoms, spring rolls, vegetarian pizza, taco sauce, chocolate, blackcurrant cordial, fizzy water etc. on top of the basic beat.

It will look like this:

1 2 3 4
Fish and chips –
1 2 3 4
sausage and beans –
1 2 3 4
poppa doms – –

You could try it as a call and response (as on the CD). One person calls out her favourite food and everyone together calls it back. Then go on to the next person.

Why we like it

- ★ It reinforces the basic beat
- ★ We find out all sorts of things about each other in a fun way
- ★ We need to listen to each other in our playing
- ★ We need to respect the person calling and not play too loud
- ★ Everyone can experience being a leader and calling

Useful tip

Sometimes people need thinking time or they suddenly forget, or they aren't feeling very confident and you find they don't come in straight away on the first beat when you think they should. This is just fine. The music goes on with everyone beating the basic beat 1 2 3 4 . This allows for thinking time and getting-it-together time. Whenever the person comes in is just fine. People may enjoy playing the basic beat but may not be ready to call. They may just like to call 'pass', or as a group you can find your own way to do a pass.

What next?

Playing together as a band seems easy, but sometimes that basic beat can be a bit all over the place. One harder challenge is to have everyone playing the basic beat on drums, table tops, percussion etc., but to have them all facing out from the circle so they can't see each other. In addition get them to close their eyes. They are now dependent on their ears and 'feeling it' to know when they are all playing the basic beat together. This can take some time but gradually, as people become more focused, so the band comes together and makes a very solid sound. There is no mistaking they are playing as one. Tape 'before' and 'after', and play it back so they can hear the difference.

Then try your 'Foodies' game again.

If you decide to use any of these games in a performance it will make such a difference to the sound you make if you are all listening to each other and really playing together as a band.

Activity 7
What's your name?

CD tracks 9 and 10

A rhythm game based on names

What you will need

★ Everyone standing or sitting in a circle
★ Body percussion e.g. hands for clapping, fingers for clicking, feet for stamping, etc
★ Percussion instruments

How to do it

Start by putting instruments down and all being ready to clap a rhythm. Go around the group checking out everyone's name and the rhythm it makes. You can start with first names and build up to full names later. So if your name is John or Anne, your rhythm is one beat. If your name is Carol or Nishat, your rhythm is two beats. Hilary and Jonathan have 3 beats, Elizabeth and Alexander have 4.

Get people with the same name rhythms to stand or sit together. Start with the single-beat group (John and Anne) and they clap that basic beat. Get each group to have a practice in turn. Then set the first group going and, once they are clapping steadily together, bring in the two-syllable names (Carol and Nishat). Their first clap will be the same as John and Anne's. Then bring in Hilary and Jonathan and everyone else. The beats look something like this…

What next?

Once you have got the hang of it, get each name-rhythm group to choose another way of playing their rhythm, e.g. finger clicks, foot stamps, tongue clicks etc. You will hear the different groups more clearly. Then pick up your instruments and play your name rhythms.

★				★			
John				John			
★	★			★	★		
Ca-	-rol			Ca-	-rol		
★	★	★		★	★	★	
Hi-	-la	-ry		Hi-	-la	-ry	
★	★	★	★	★	★	★	★
Al-	-ex	-and	-er	Al-	-ex	-and	-er

Why we like it

- ★ You use your name to make a rhythm, so it is very familiar
- ★ The results of combining the rhythms can sound fantastic
- ★ If you get confused and play a different rhythm it really doesn't matter!

Useful tip

Start with these regular beats to keep it simple. You can move on to different rhythms of names once you get the hang of this. Listen to the CD track 10 and hear different ways to say the rhythms of John, Carol, Hilary and Elizabeth.

You can play 'Orchestration' (see activity 13 in this section), conducting the different groups to play louder, softer etc. You can move around. You can use full names so the rhythms get more complicated.

Soundbite on What's your name?

To help one group who struggled with this activity we got into groups with one name, so there were four people who were the 'John' group, and four who were the 'Lisa' group, and another four who were the 'Rhiannon' group. They were all focused on the same name and rhythm and helped each other to keep in time.

Activity 8
All about eight

CD track 11

Rhythm games based on a count of eight

What you will need

★ Instruments or be ready to clap

How to do it

The first game, 'After eight' starts as a simple version of 'Copy me do' (activity 10 in this section). You play eight beats on your drum and everyone responds to you by playing eight beats on their instruments.

Once you have got this perfect (it can take a little practice!) you tell the group: 'Fours', and beat four beats to which they respond with four beats. Do this for a bit, then reduce to two beats and then one. At any time you can call with eight, four, two or one and the response should match.

Once you get really good at this, you can move on to 'Finish the eight'. You play any number of beats between one and eight, and the group has to play the rest to finish the eight. So if you play 4 beats, they play 4; if you play 6 beats, they play 2; if you play 3 beats, they play 5.

Ideally there are no gaps between the eights. It takes a lot of concentration!

Why we like it

★ It starts off simply
★ It is good practice for counting together and keeping in time
★ It requires concentration
★ It can become very challenging
★ When you are all in rhythm with a basic beat it sounds very exciting and can be exhilarating to play

Useful tip

Watch out for speeding up – it's easy to get carried away!

What next?

The simple version of this activity works well for carnivals, see section 4, activity 6.

Soundbite on After eight

We used the 'After eight' game as a performance. Beginning with the eight beat call and response we went to four and then two and then one, then one again (this repetition brings an added excitement to the game) and back to eight. This was the structure: 8, 4, 2, 1, 1, 8, 4, 2, 1, 1, etc (as on the CD). In the performance, on each repetition of the game a different person did the calling so we heard different instrument solos, and also on each repetition we got faster so by the end it was very exciting.

Activity 9
Number one to number five

CD track 12

What you will need

★ Everyone sitting or standing in a circle
★ A drum or other instrument or object to beat

How to do it

Everyone needs to have a number before the game can start. Begin with yourself as the leader and call yourself number 1, saying it out loud, and then number people off round the circle....2 3 4 5 6 etc.

Play a strong and steady basic beat – 1 2 3 4 – on your drum, table tops, resonance board, wheelchair, tray etc. This is the first step, the foundation of the wall. Keep it going continually.

Then as number 1 you begin by calling over the top of the basic beat and passing the beat onto another number in the group like this:

number 1 to number 8

Number 8 immediately picks up the chant and calls

number 8 to number 4
or whichever number is chosen by number 8.

Number 4 then picks up the chant and calls:

number 4 to number 12 etc.

Continue with this pattern until you have called everyone's number.

Why we like it?

★ It hones our listening skills
★ It reinforces the basic beat
★ It's great for a carnival (see section 4, activity 6)
★ We can add layers of percussion and liven it up

Useful tip

Sometimes people are caught out and can't remember their number so they don't come in straight away on the first beat when you think they should. This is just fine. The music goes on with everyone beating the basic beat 1 2 3 4. This allows for thinking time and getting-it-together time. Whenever they come in is just fine.

What next?

Once people are confident with the game try it a little faster; and then a little faster and a little faster!! Try it using handclaps or finger clicks.

Try moving it round the room – so you really have to listen to the number called and remember your own.

For those who are ready for a bit of extra fun, if you miss your number or forget to come in you have to forfeit something…!

Soundbite on Number one to number five

We were working with a youth group, preparing for a performance for family and friends. Everyone was sitting in a circle and had a percussion instrument by their feet. When someone's number was called that person picked up her instrument, at the same time continuing the chant and calling someone else's number. She then played her percussion and kept playing for the rest of the game. Gradually more instruments were added so by the end of the chant everyone was playing in the band.

It was very effective and everyone learned not to play too loudly so the number calls could be heard. Once everyone was in they could play as loud as they liked.

Activity 10
Copy me do

CD track 13

Play your own individual rhythms on your instruments and lead the 'band'

What you will need

- ★ Instruments
- ★ Space to sit or stand in a circle

How to do it

Make sure everyone has had time to play around on their instruments to see what sounds they can make with them and what rhythms they can play. When you are ready, call a stop. Play a simple rhythm on your instrument and ask everyone to give it back to you by copying it. Do it again, about four times, so that everyone gets a chance to hear it and play it. A really simple way to start is to play either 1 2 or 3 beats for the group to play back to you. (Listen to the first part of track 13 on the CD.)

Now you can make this into the 'Copy me do' game. Begin with everyone playing the basic beat (see activity 3 in this section) on their instruments. When you think they are ready, conduct them to play more quietly so they can hear your 'rhythm call' on top. Do as you did before, playing a rhythm for people to copy. When you have finished, raise your hand so everyone knows you have finished. Then all play the basic beat again until another 'caller' comes forward by raising her hand so that everyone knows who will be leading the next rhythm call. Tell people to play their rhythm at least four times. They can play the same rhythm four times or they could change it each time if they want.

Why we like it

- ★ We get to hear and play lots of different rhythms
- ★ We get to hear the sound of a variety of instruments
- ★ We learn to listen carefully
- ★ We learn to respect each other's contribution
- ★ Individuals have an opportunity to shine

- ★ It boosts confidence
- ★ A great carnival activity as you can walk around at the same time as playing

What next?

You can very quickly make this into a performance by deciding on the order of the callers and just going for one call and response after another. You can add to the interest by the caller playing loud or soft and everyone copying the dynamics.

Look at the activities in section 3 – Finding Your Voice – and try activity 3 to play this game using your voice.

Useful tip

It is very easy to come in too soon and not listen to the whole of the caller's rhythm. This can be fun but as you get better and better at listening you will enjoy the music-making more if you let the caller finish.

Soundbite on Copy me do

We spent one day working with a group of 12-year-olds and they had to perform at the end of the day. This turned out to be a great activity for them. All those who wanted to play on their own could, and those who just loved playing as a 'band' could do that too. It didn't matter at all that some people couldn't remember what rhythm to play, as this meant the 'band's' composition was always fresh and new.

We helped some people who couldn't think of a rhythm by playing 'Foodies' (activity 5 in this section) for inspiration.

For other ideas on making performances from a game see section 4, activity 5.

Drum roll on rhythm

We often find ourselves tapping our toes, tapping the steering wheel in the car, feeling the beat of music and wanting to move. This is not at all surprising considering we spent nine months before we were born listening to and feeling the regular pulse in the womb. Rhythm is an integral part of our lives both outside us and within. Every culture has its own rhythm and everyone has a personal rhythm. Rhythm gives order to sound and movement. Even though leaves and rain don't fall in a particular time, they have their own rhythm. Feel your heartbeat in your neck or wrist. Use your voice to mimic your heartbeat. What does it sound like? THUD DUB, THUD DUB.

From birth we develop an awareness of time's patterns. Activities begin and end, there is time for activity and rest and we experience sound and silence.

The phrasing and pattern of life is determined by natural events like day and night, light and dark, tides and seasons.

These factors shape and make sense of our lives. The first small pattern of our heartbeat later on relates to early language, e.g. Mama, Dada, hungry. We move on and phrase words together into sentences to make meaning but still intersperse these with short silences by taking breaths at commas and full stops. Music can be another language for us to use, a language filled with rhythm and silences phrased and put together in much the same way. We are born to enjoy and make rhythm… so let's do it.

Activity 11
Beat, beat, beat upon the tom-tom!

CD track 14

Playing with a sound poem

What you will need

- ⋆ Everyone sitting in a circle
- ⋆ A drum or several drums

How to do it

Listen to the poem on the CD so you can hear how it fits with the basic beat. There are two verses to the poem, with the beginning of the first verse repeated at the end. Both verses use a strong basic beat but the first verse lends itself to very strong marching, actions or dance movements while the second verse said very quietly is good for freer movements and actions (see soundbite).

Here is the sound poem. Each line is chanted over 4 beats and you can hear on the CD how each of the words 'beat' has a beat to itself.

1 2 3 4
Beat beat beat upon the tom-tom
Beat beat beat upon the drum
Beat beat beat upon the tom-tom
Beat beat beat upon the drum

Shuffle to the left, shuffle to the left
Shuffle shuffle shuffle shuffle, shuffle
to the left
Shuffle to the right, shuffle to the right
Shuffle shuffle shuffle shuffle, shuffle
to the right

AND
Beat beat beat upon the tom-tom
Beat beat beat upon the drum
Beat beat beat upon the tom-tom
Beat beat beat upon the drum

Begin by playing a strong steady beat – 1 2 3 4 – on your drums. Keep it going continually.

Chant the first verse together loudly and definitely. At the end of the first verse just take a couple of seconds for a silence to help denote a change is coming. Then begin to chant the second verse very quietly; and instead of drumming just rumble quietly with your fingertips on your drums to the left and then to the right. At the end of that verse immediately shout out 'AND …' going straight into the first verse again with a good strong, steady basic beat on your drums.

Why we like it

- ★ You can move it in your body and really feel that basic beat
- ★ It is so simple but very effective
- ★ You can split into two groups
- ★ You can change the words of the second verse and try different actions and movements (see soundbite).
- ★ It is very exciting to play

Soundbite on Beat, beat, beat upon the tom-tom!

A group of nursery children were playing this. We used some bongos and small drums with beaters. Those who didn't have drums beat their knees. I got up in the middle of the circle inviting a few children to join me. I made sure there was another adult there to keep the strong basic beat for the poem. For the first verse we danced with powerful, warrior-like movements. In the second verse I encouraged the group to form a little huddle, and we just shuffled one way and then the other, gently pushing each other until we ended up falling over on top of each other with much hilarity. Then the group came in with the strong first verse again and it refocused our attention: we got up and danced our strong, warrior movements once more. It was a wonderful experience of being free and doing something a bit 'naughty', but having it contained in the strong basic beat of the chant's first verse.

In another setting the teacher who had learned this chant on one of our workshops took the children outside on an autumn day: they beat their drums and chanted around a pile of autumn leaves. On the second verse a few children went into the middle of the leaves and 'shuffled' around in them, fell into them, threw them into the air and on the return to the first verse they joined the circle again. It took a few goes but gradually the beat became the containment for the freer activity. They called it 'The Autumn Leaves Shuffle'

What next?

Try taking the chant outside and change the second verse to:

> Run away and hide, run away and hide
> Run, run, run, run, run away and hide etc

On the repeat of the first verse the children could come out of their hiding places and march back to where you began, or you could go round and collect them with your drum, rather like the Pied Piper, and march back to the starting place.

Activity 12
Rhythm whispers

A game just like Chinese whispers only using body rhythms!

What you will need

- ★ Yourselves
- ★ Space to stand in lines

How to do it

Everyone stands in a line one behind the other but not too close together. The leader is at the back of the line and makes a rhythm on the back of the person in front. You can use your fingers, palms, knuckles or fists but keep it simple at first. This person then repeats the rhythm on the back of the person in front of her and so on down the line to the front. The person at the back who invented the rhythm moves to the side where everyone can see her, and the last person to get the rhythm comes and makes it on her back. Was it the same? The leader now shows the group what the original rhythm was, to see how it changed on the way down the line.

Why we like it

- ★ Feeling a rhythm is often a new experience
- ★ Practice at being accurate with rhythms
- ★ There is a degree of suspense
- ★ You have to concentrate

Useful tip

It is good to ask everyone if they are comfortable with being touched and having their back played.

What next?

If you have a big group and they are able to keep their eyes closed without speaking it's great to stand in a circle to pass the rhythm on.

You can also try this as a team game. Let's say there are three teams. One person from each team comes to you to receive 'the rhythm' that will be passed on. At a signal they go back to their group and begin to pass the rhythm down the line.

Once the rhythm has made it all the way to the front in each team, the three people at the front of the lines come forward and show everyone the rhythm they received. They could play it all at once or one at a time. Then choose another rhythm and new people to begin passing it on.

Drum roll on touch

Our sense of touch shows us the shape, size and 'feel' of our world.

We learn to avoid touching something hot, a sharp edge or point, or very cold metal. Touch keeps us safe. We feel happy when we stroke a dog, or when we get a hug. We feel sad when we run into something hard or fall over.

The organ used in touching is the skin. Every bit of skin all over our bodies, including our nails, is used for touching. The skin is the largest sensory organ in the body. It is covered in numerous receptors that receive information from the outside environment. The sensory receptors of the skin are concerned with at least five different senses: pain, heat, cold, touch, and pressure. The nerve endings in the skin send signals to the brain; the brain analyses the signals and registers the effect of the touch, then signals the reaction to the rest of the body.

Not everyone likes to be touched and you may have such people in your group. Some people react negatively to touch. Some sections of the skin are more sensitive than others and some people are much more sensitive to touch than other people. Some people with profound learning difficulties who are also wheelchair users get less 'feedback' from people through touch, outside of their daily care routine. Activities like 'Rhythm whispers' provide opportunities for appropriate and fun touch.

Ultimately it is a question of being gentle, careful, knowing your group and respecting each other by asking first if people mind being touched.

Activity 13
Body Rhythms

A 'pass it on' game using body percussion

How to do it

Start with yourself only in the room and everyone else outside with their fingers in their ears! Decide on a rhythm to play using your body: e.g. feet stamps, knee-knocks and finger clicks – not too complicated to begin with. It might help to make rhythms around food or drinks or a sentence (see activity 6 in this section). Invite another person in. She will stand facing you and watch and listen to you play your body rhythms. She doesn't play it back but invites another person in, in turn repeating the rhythm using the same body parts, passing it onto the new person in the room who becomes the next caller – and so on.

Once everyone is back in the room and has had a go at calling the rhythm, the last person repeats it for the person who made it up in the first place.

Why we like it

- ★ It encourages our listening and observation skills
- ★ We soon see who finds it easier to listen or watch
- ★ We find out what wonderful instruments our bodies are
- ★ We discover amazing new rhythms
- ★ We become more confident at making up rhythms

What next?

You can add a challenge by asking people to listen to the rhythm without looking. From here you can go on to play the 'Pile up' game (activity 14 in this section), using all the different rhythms that came out of your listening and watching; and lo and behold you have an amazing composition.

Useful tips

You can make the game very simple to begin with by using just claps and clicks.

Tapping, sweeping, scraping, sliding, knocking, clapping, stamping, clicking, flicking, rubbing, are just some of the ways to play your body. It is important to show your group just which body parts are appropriate to use in this game. You can do this by playing a 'Copy me do' game (activity 10 in this section). Begin with the caller scraping feet on the floor, and when everyone is doing this move onto another one, e.g. running on tiptoes or rubbing your knees or clicking your tongue etc.

Activity 14
Pile up

CD track 15

Making music together as a 'band' is often a new experience for people. This game enables everyone to do just that regardless of their music-making experience or ability. A new composition is made every time you play the game.

What you will need

- ★ Space to sit in a circle and any drums and percussion instruments you have made or bought. Even your air guitars!

How to do it

In the beginning the group leader will be the most important person in the music-making. She will play the strong, steady, basic beat that holds the whole composition together. It is best if you have a drum with a good strong sound.

Start playing a steady basic beat 1 2 3 4 and keep this going. When you think everyone has heard your wonderful playing and the 'band' is focused, invite the player to your left to join the band by looking at her 'meaningfully'.

This person then joins the band and plays her instrument on top of your basic beat. She can keep the basic beat too if she wants, or try her own rhythm on top. There are now two players in the band.

When the second player thinks the rest of the band has heard your 'duet' and how well you play together, the next person to the left is invited to join the band: the second player likewise looks 'meaningfully' at this next person, who joins in with her shaker, drum or other instrument. The rest of the band now listen to this trio.

Continue to pile up the rhythms until everyone in the band is playing.

Just enjoy listening to all those rhythms and keep playing for as long as you want to. Remember the picture of the brick wall with all the layers? (See the drum roll for activity 3 in this section.) By the end you will have as many layers on your wall as there are players.

Use an agreed drum rhythm to stop or the familiar a... a... a... and STOP!

If you like, give yourselves an Umfolosi Ulu! (See the drum roll in section 5, activity 3, and listen to track 16 on the CD.)

Why we like it

- ★ You can play in a band for the first time
- ★ The music-making is unique every time you play the game
- ★ Everyone can join in, there is a role for all
- ★ It encourages concentration and listening to each other
- ★ It develops confidence
- ★ There is no music to read
- ★ You can play it round the resonance board

Useful tips

It helps to have played lots of other rhythm games in this section first.

When you first play 'Pile up' keep the rhythms simple.

If someone is unsure about what to play let them know they can join you on the basic beat – the most important, underlying beat. When they are feeling confident they can try their own rhythm out and return to the basic beat whenever they want to.

Some people find it hard to sit still, so standing, playing and moving is great.

What next?

You can play 'Foodies' (section 2 activity 6) or 'What's Your Name?' (section 2 activity 7) as a pile up.

Once your composition is in full swing go on to play the game 'Orchestration' (activity 15 in this section). The combination of both games gives you a great way to perform without having to practise a lot first.

A challenge for this game is to pile up the rhythms randomly. Once you as leader have established the basic beat, look at any person in the group to invite her to play. This means everyone has to be watching very carefully to see who is the next person to play. This can be quite tricky.

Instead of calling a STOP at the end, try 'piling down' your composition round the circle; or if you want a challenge, pile down randomly. You are left at the end with just the basic beat. If the leader fades this out it gives a very powerful ending. (You will hear a pile down on the CD.)

Try 'Pile up' on the resonance boards for people to have a physical experience of the growing sound. It is also very effective to simply pile up a rumble (see activity 2 in this section) and pile it down again. This is particularly good for children and young people with profound and complex needs.

Soundbite on Pile up

We have played this game so many times with a wide variety of groups. It is so exciting to see people filled with pleasure at playing in a band for the first time. Some comments we have had are: 'That was awesome', ' I never knew I could do that', 'I want to do that again and again and again.'

We have also played this game around the resonance boards, creating an environment of sound for children and young people who have profound and complex needs. They are able to experience the build-up of the music and all the different rhythms people choose to play.

In a workshop with a group of young adults with learning difficulties, we enabled one young man to take part by pre-recording some percussion on a 'switch'. When he wanted he could press the switch and join in at any time. He also chose which percussion sounds he wanted on the switch.

Drum roll on making an environment of sound

It is often difficult to feel you are successfully including all people in your music-making, especially those who are unable to clap their hands independently, dance, hold or play an instrument or sing songs.

We believe it is just as important for these people to experience an environment of sound and rhythm: to be and not necessarily to do. To listen, feel and enjoy with no expectation, to hold an instrument, clap hands or visibly join in.

Everyone in the session is part of the music-making, whoever is in the group – teachers, learning support assistants, nursery nurses, play workers, parents, children etc. Everyone's input is important and forms the content of that group. Input may well involve just enjoying the experience of being surrounded by sound and rhythm and being given an opportunity in the silence to express this enjoyment vocally or with one's body. The sounds or movement which participants offer become part of the song, chant or dance.

It is up to us to play around with all the activities in this book to create different environments of sound so everyone can enjoy and be part of music-making activities.

One effective way of making an 'environment of sound' is to play the next game in this section, 'Orchestration'.

Activity 15
Orchestration

Giving shape and form to your music-making

What you need

- ⋆ Space to sit in a circle
- ⋆ Percussion instruments and drums

How to do it

Begin by playing together as a band. The easiest way to do this is to play 'Pile up' (see activity 12 in this section).
Once everyone is playing, make sure one of the other players now has responsibility for the basic beat, and go into the middle of the circle, where you become the conductor. As conductor, you will use your face, hands and body to orchestrate and shape the music your band is playing. Begin by turning around slowly in the middle of the circle making sure everyone is looking at you. Point to your eyes to show that this is what you need people to do.

Now try these simple and effective conducting techniques:

A. Getting quiet
Bring your arms out to the side of you, palms down. Slowly bring your arms down as you also bend your knees and move

your body down to the floor. At the same time use your eyes, keeping them alert, so as to keep people's attention. Use your mouth to form a silent 'sssh'. Miraculously your band will play more quietly.

B. Getting louder
Bring your arms out to the side palms up. Raise your arms up slowly and stand on tiptoe. Raise your arms as high as they can go and also raise your eyebrows.

C. Stopping the whole band
Point to your eyes to make sure people know they need to watch you. Turn round slowly in the middle with your arm out and your finger pointed at people, at about waist height. This is to let people know this instruction is for the whole band. Lift one arm up high with your fingers in a fist. With large movements open out your thumb and at the same time silently say '1' with exaggerated mouth movements. Then open out the next finger and silently say '2'. Then the next finger and say '3'. Then the next finger and say '4'. Then raise both arms up, palms facing forward, and make a stop sign, as you silently say 'Stop'.

Your whole band will stop. To make the following silence exciting and very effective count to 8 silently, but with exaggerated mouth movements so people can see; and then bring the band in again as at D. below.

D. Starting the whole band
Lift one arm up high with your fingers in a fist. With large movements open out your thumb and at the same time silently say '1' with exaggerated mouth movements. Then open out the next finger and silently say '2'. Then the next finger and say '3'. Then the next finger and say '4'. Then bring your arms in front as if you were going to fold them and make a rolling motion, one forearm and hand over the other like John Travolta in 'Saturday Night Fever', or the children's song 'Wind the Bobbin Up.' Everyone begins playing again.

This is such fun you can stop and start several times for effect.

E. Getting faster
This is a great way to finish your whole orchestrated piece. Use your body to show moving in slow motion, then gradually speed up. Mouth the word 'faster' so your orchestra plays faster as you speed up. As the music-making begins to lose its rhythm and is sounding a bit chaotic you can really let go and shake your whole body, run on the spot till everyone is shaking their shakers madly and drumming their drums with all their might. Then use our vocal stop very loudly, together with the hand stop above, and call a…a…a…and STOP! Wow!

Why we like it

- ⋆ Everyone can conduct and experience the power-trip of a lifetime
- ⋆ It develops your observation and listening skills
- ⋆ You experience the variety of dynamics involved in music-making
- ⋆ You understand how music is made more interesting
- ⋆ You can control a band of music makers
- ⋆ You can hear different percussion instruments, especially those that make very small sounds

What next?

Now you have the basics you can play around with these to sculpt your composition. Try the following:

- ★ Just have the drums play. Walk round the inside of the band and stop each player in turn who isn't playing a drum by just holding your hand up in a stop sign. To each of the drum players do the John Travolta hand roll to tell them they are to keep playing. Then listen. Do you like it? How can you change it?
- ★ You can then bring other percussion back in by pointing to it and doing the hand roll. You can stop the drums and just have shakers, or metal sounds, or wooden sounds
- ★ You can have one half of the band playing quietly and the other loudly, and then swap them round
- ★ You can stop one half of the band so they can listen to the others
- ★ If some people are playing percussion with a very gentle sound it is a great opportunity to hear just the soft sounds that drums otherwise drown out
- ★ If at any stage you are bowled over by how fantastic you sound or are simply enjoying yourselves, don't forget to let rip with the 'Umfolosi Ulu' (see drum roll in section 5, activity 3, and listen to track 16 on the CD).
- ★ If you are the conductor in the middle you can sit down at any time and invite another conductor to go into the middle and 'do her thing'.

Useful tip

If at any time you are unsure about what to do, or no one wants to conduct, or it is getting a bit chaotic, or the pace is too slow, remember you can stop it at any time and start again when you are ready or have made any changes you want.

For conductors who might find organising their body in this way a little too difficult, have some cue cards for them to use, showing pictures of the percussion instruments such as drums, shakers, wooden instruments and metal instruments. Also have a stop and go sign and a getting louder and getting quieter sound card. They can then choose a card and, perhaps with help, initially hold up the cards to tell people what they want to do.

Soundbite on orchestration

We were working with a youth group and they decided they wanted to play the orchestration game for a performance piece. One of the conductors, a young Asian lad, came into the middle and proceeded to move his arms in Indian dance style which meant that for one half of the band his arm was up with his palm up so they played loud, and for the other half his arm was down with the palm down so they played soft. Then he simply switched his arms around as is done in Asian dances and the dynamics of each half of the band swapped over too. It was very effective.

Drum roll on orchestration

The effects possible with your composition are no different from those made by a conductor leading a symphony orchestra. The latter uses the same elements, such as dynamics, tempo, timbre, texture and structure in music-making, though often at a more sophisticated level. However, the more you play this game and play around with it, the more sophisticated you will find your own conducting becoming and the resulting music will get better and better. Just remember to listen to your music-making and enjoy the different sounds without judging the end result as good or bad. It is all great. Remember to congratulate yourselves.

By playing this game you have will been creating amazing environments of sound (see drum roll for activity 12 in this section).

Activity 16
Walking on the wall

A game for individuals to 'shine' with their rhythms.

What you need

- ★ Space to sit in a circle, your drums and percussion instruments.

How you do it

Begin by playing together as a band. The easiest way to do this is to play game 13 in this section, 'Pile up'. Once everyone is playing, invite someone to go 'walking on the wall'. This is where one person plays her own solo on top of the band's playing.

When a soloist has come forward, perhaps by saying 'me' or putting her hand up, conduct the band to play softly (see 'Orchestration', activity 14 in this section).

The soloist then takes the spotlight and plays as if she was the lead player of the band, and as though people are there just to listen to her. Once she has finished she can indicate this by putting her hand up or simply joining the rest of the band and playing quietly with them. Now the rest of the band must give her an 'Umfolosi Ulu' – CD track 16 – to show appreciation for her magnificent playing.

Carry on playing as a band and invite another soloist.

Why we like it

- ★ It gives everyone the opportunity to play solo
- ★ It's great for those who want to play drums in a loud and fancy way, especially boys
- ★ You learn to appreciate different instruments and the sounds they make

- ★ You learn to listen to and appreciate diversity of playing
- ★ It gives those who don't want to play solo a very important part in the band

Useful tip

Those who continually choose to play drums are often the ones who really want to play solo and imitate their favourite kit-drum player. These are often boys. This is a prime opportunity for them to do so. However, so that everyone feels they can have a go and have an opportunity to 'shine' even if they are playing an instrument with a smaller sound, you might like to play the game on one occasion as 'Walking on the wall for drum solos' and another time as 'Walking on the wall for other percussion solos'. As everyone increasingly comes to appreciate the diversity of instruments and players you can mix the solos up.

Safety notes

There will always be people for whom the idea of soloing is far too scary. Make sure everyone knows you don't have to solo, and that playing in the band supporting the soloist is equally important.

What next?

People will soon become very proficient at doing their solos. A little more challenging is to ask the person about to solo to sit first without playing, with eyes closed and just listen to the rest of the band. Listening to these rhythms, she can think a little more about what would sound good on top of them. There may be a space that she might want to put a particular sound or rhythm into, or she may want to make sure that a space remains a space. After this time for reflection and 'tuning in', the solo begins.

Try beginning with the 'Pile up' game, followed by the 'Orchestration' game and finally 'Walking on the wall'. You could finish with the last part of the Orchestration game, getting faster and faster until everyone is playing loudly and fast; and then STOP it!

Drum roll on Walking on the wall

This structure of providing a space for people to play their solos is very much part of the jazz tradition where the band plays together and then each instrumentalist has a spot to improvise and show off her talents. Most of us want to have a go at this too. 'Walking on the wall' allows for everyone to experience this.

The band playing underneath the soloist provides the wall's foundation and supports the soloist to prevent her 'falling off'. If at any time the soloist begins to 'fall' she can climb down a layer and simply play the basic beat or a more simple rhythm with the rest of the band. She can then climb back up the wall and go solo again if she wants.

Section 3

Finding Your Voice

Activity 1
Warm up your body

CD track 17

Releasing tension and getting the body moving before singing and chanting

What you will need

★ Space for everyone to stand in a circle
★ Space to spread out and stretch your arms wide

How to do it

This is a series of exercises you can use to gently warm up your group physically before you warm up their voices. Of course you can use any simple exercises you are familiar with; this is just a starting point.

1. Begin by standing straight and tall, feet a few centimetres apart and parallel. Imagine a thread is pulling the top of your head towards the ceiling, helping you to make your spine longer. Let your shoulders relax. Notice your breathing, listen to it and feel how it moves your body.

2. Gently turn your head to look over your right shoulder, keeping the chin parallel to the floor. Slowly return to face forwards, then gently turn to the left. Repeat this three times, on both sides.

3. Gently stretch the left side of your neck so that your right ear moves towards your shoulder. Don't lift the shoulder. Slowly straighten up, then stretch the right side of your neck, allowing your left ear to move towards your left shoulder. Repeat three times, both sides.

4. Rotate your shoulders, bringing them forwards, then up, back, then down. Repeat five times then rotate in the opposite direction.

5. Squeeze your shoulders towards the ears then gently lower them.

6. Raise your arms over the head and stretch your fingertips towards the ceiling. Gently lower. Repeat, going up on tiptoes for a really big stretch, come down slowly.

7. Have the legs about 15 cm apart. Place the hands on the thighs and gradually slide them down the legs towards the floor. Hang there! Slowly come up, uncurling so that your head is the last thing to be raised. Repeat three times.

8. Choose a consonant letter of the alphabet. Shake your right hand towards the centre of the circle and on each shake say the *sound* of your letter (e.g. for the letter ‘t’ say tuh not tee) Do this eight times, fast. Choose a different letter for the left hand, right leg and left leg. Watch out for letter ‘F’!

9. Get everyone to shake all over!

10. Work on faces. Open your mouth and eyes as wide as possible and look around the circle. Then screw your face up as tight as you can. Do this several times.

11. Pretend you are chewing a small piece of chewing gum… now imagine it is bigger… now pretend it is a huge piece of sticky toffee. (This will warm up the jaw area!)

12. Stretch your arms up and out to the sides, yawn if you need to. Now you are ready to warm up your voice.

Why we like it

★ Tension in the shoulders and neck can prevent the voice from working well, releasing tension can protect the voice

★ Apart from the physical benefits of preparing your body, doing these exercises together will focus the group

★ You don’t have to be really serious as you do this, it can make people laugh, especially the face exercises

★ People are often more willing to do exercises which don’t involve them making much noise than those which do. Physical exercises before vocal ones can build up confidence

Safety notes

Tell your group to look after themselves and not strain. Tell them that if anything feels uncomfortable they should not do it. These are gentle warm-up exercises, not competitive sport. Stress the need to move slowly where stated in the descriptions above.

What next?

Move on to activity 2, warming up your voice!

Drum roll on movement

When we sing it is not just our mouth and vocal cords which do the work. Crucial to the sound is the breath; and to breathe deeply and effectively our bodies need to be relaxed. Simply focusing on your own breath and slowing it down by gently increasing the length of your out-breath can be excellent preparation for singing. Our whole body is linked to the sounds we make when we sing. Gentle movements can keep you relaxed and help you to feel a rhythm. As well as the shoulders and neck mentioned above, we often have lots of tension in our legs, especially our knees. It can really free the voice if you relax the knees, bend them slightly and allow movement to happen naturally. You can imagine you are standing up to your waist in warm water, gently bobbing with the current.

Activity 2
Warm up your voice

CD track 18

Protecting your voice and building confidence before singing and chanting

What you will need

- ★ Space for everyone to stand in a circle

How to do it

After warming up your body, it's time to warm up your voice.

1. Stand comfortably with your feet apart and release any tension in your knees – try squeezing the muscles in the knees and then letting them go.

2. Take a deep breath in and then gently hum as you breathe out. Repeat 3 times, don't strain to hold the note but try to let the air out slowly so that the humming gets a bit longer each time.

3. Use your hand to indicate a lift going up and down. Tell the group to imagine they are providing sound effects for a little fly caught in the lift. As they hum they should slide the note higher when you lift your hand, and lower when you lower your hand. Move your hand quite slowly at first, speed up as they get the hang of it!

4. You hold your fist clenched. Explain to the group that they will start humming and when you open your hand they should open their mouths so that the hum changes to an 'ahhh'. The first time you do this it will probably be quite quiet. Remind the group of the exercise they did where they opened their mouths wide (exercise 10 in last activity). Repeat the hum to 'ahh' exercise with wide mouths and observe the difference. Important – if you open your mouth more, more sound comes out!

5. Repeat the above exercise but ask the group to try to make the 'ahh' sound spooky – they don't need to scream or shout, but just choose a note that sounds eerie. Give it a try – together you will make a fabulous (some might say awful!) discordant sound. Add scary postures if you want to (pull faces, make claw hands etc.)

6. Make sounds together. You can try saying words over and over again, in rhythm with each other. Try 'ticky tacky' or 'lu la lu la' or 'crunchy crisps'. Simple combinations of words with a different vowel will get the voice and face working. You can all be fire engines 'nee naw, nee naw', or blow air through loose lips and sound like horses! Other animal sounds can be good too – moo, baa, quack! It doesn't really matter what you do as long as you do it together, make a noise and have fun!

Why we like it

- ★ If you are going to sing then it is wise to warm up your vocal cords – this way is fun at the same time.
- ★ Making noises all together is much less intimidating than singing straight away.
- ★ If you are feeling nervous about letting any sound out, there is no pressure to stay in tune or make a 'nice sound'.
- ★ It leads you gently into coordinating the sound you make in the following activities.
- ★ It will get the group focusing and listening before you move on to anything more complicated.

Safety notes

Remind the group they are warming up their voices so they should treat them gently and not strain or hurt them in any way.

What next?

You are ready to move on to other activities in this section!

Soundbite on warm-ups

Sometimes the idea of a warm-up can engage a group – likening it to the way you warm up for sports can make it an accessible concept for sporty types who may be sceptical about music games. For others it sounds a bit boring and they just want to get on with it… in that case call it something else like 'waking up your voice' or 'super sounds' or anything else you like!

Drum roll on the voice

You have the gift of an instrument – your voice. The voice you have now is the voice you will always have, it will never change into a different voice. If you can't get within miles of Stevie Wonder's high notes now, you probably never will (although practice certainly can extend your vocal range). This is important to know, so you don't feel you can't sing just because you can't get certain notes in a song that you like.

It may be helpful to know how the sound of your voice is produced. When you talk or sing, your vocal cords contract in a certain fashion, and as you breathe out the air passes through them, making them vibrate. This action produces sound. By using the tongue and lips this sound is shaped into words, high and low sounds, grunts, animal imitations or whatever you want to do. Then the sound needs amplifiying. The sound of a piano or guitar is not made by the strings alone. Every instrument has an amplifier. In the case of the acoustic guitar this is the resonating space inside the body of the instrument. In the human voice it is the space inside you. The basic sound is made by the vocal cords and this is made louder by the 'tunnel' of your throat, the domed shape of your mouth and the space inside your head. That is why humming is so good – you can feel the resonance behind your nose. Hmmmmmmmm!

Absolutely essential to this process is the way we use our ears to really hear the different sounds. No doubt you have heard of people who 'play by ear' or 'sing by ear'. Games and activities which enhance our ability to hear are therefore also very useful for singing.

Activity 3
Repeat after me

CD tracks 19 and 20

A game to gently start the group singing

What you will need

★ Everyone warmed up and in a circle
★ Some ideas to get things started

How to do it

Start by 'Legging it' (section 2, activity 3) to get everyone moving to a basic beat. Then all you do is sing, shout or say something and the group repeats it back to you. You can simply say 'hello' or 'ready?' to start with, so no one feels they are singing. Play with the volume and tone of your voice – make it loud, soft, whisper, be squeaky or deep, use an accent and, as the group relaxes into copying you, you can introduce more singing. 'La, la, la' or 'wey o' on any notes are good starting points. Listen to the CD track 19 for more inspiration!

Why we like it

★ You can start singing without the pressure of learning a song
★ Everyone joins in together and the phrases are short, so not too intimidating
★ You can pass the leadership round (see 'what next?' below)
★ Taking the lead is a great confidence booster
★ It really doesn't matter what sound you make – everyone copies it regardless!

Useful tip

You can use the structure of a song to get you started if you prefer. On the CD you will find 'Vi, Vo, Vista' track 20 which has a clear sequence of calls which you can adapt and change to fit your theme, group or mood!

What next?

Once you have got the pattern going, you can pass the

leadership around your circle. We usually set up a signal so when you are ready to pass the leadership on, you touch the arm of the person next to you. When it is your turn you can carry on as long as you like, and if you don't want to lead at all you just touch the arm of the person the other side of you and pass the leadership on.

Soundbite on Repeat after me

A voice workshop leader used an adaptation of this game and called it 'hoeing'. Instead of 'Legging it', everyone put one foot towards the centre of the circle and used their arms to mime a hoeing action. We were reminded of how people used to sing as they carried out manual work, and this image inspired our calls to each other. The action kept us in time without the sound of stepping. If you do this, make sure you change position after a while and lead with the other side of your body so that you don't start to ache on one side. Try this action with the 'Ungawa' chant. CD track 27.

Drum roll on singing

Singing is good for you. Anyone who can hear can sing – even if you think you can't sing in tune or think you are tone deaf. Many of us have been discouraged from singing early in life – perhaps by not being selected for the school choir, or by being told to stand at the back and just mouth the words. We often think music is outside us, and that to make music we need to be able to play an instrument. But our first instrument is our voice and body. From a very early age we use these together with the natural rhythm within us to engage in music making and respond to music.

Community singing has been replaced by television, computer games and digitalised music. People used to sing at home, in sing-alongs at the village pub, at village festivals, alongside brass bands or in the church choir. Perhaps the best informal singing we participate in now is on the terraces at a football match, or at the local Karaoke session, or when celebrating Burns' Night.

Research shows that children who sing happily and more or less in tune by the age of five have been sung to by their mothers from an early age. Very recent research shows that when mothers sing to their babies they feel much better in themselves and about themselves.

Singing has proven emotional, physiological, intellectual and aesthetic benefits.

So get singing!

Activity 4
Sound bath

CD track 21

An improvisation game that will give you the feeling of being in a bath of sound, surrounded by vocal sounds made in the moment. A new composition every time.

What you will need

★ Just yourselves and your voices

How to do it

Make sure you have sung lots of songs and chants before trying this game. You will know when your group is confident enough to play around a bit with the endless variety of vocal sounds and body percussion that we can make.

Tell the group that the music they are about to make is unique, that you don't yet know what will happen or how it will sound and that whatever happens will be great.

You will need to explain the following.

Remind them of the 'Pile up' game – section 2, activity 13. This will be a similar structure but using vocal sounds.

You start by playing a soft, basic beat on a drum, table or your knees Then make a sound with your voice on top of the basic beat. (you could hum, say bbbbb or use words like zzzip or pitter patter for example.) As you can hear on the CD you don't have to make a continuous sound, in fact if you leave gaps it gives the next person an opportunity to make his sound in the space.

When you are ready, look at the person next to you so he knows it is his turn to make a sound. Keep your sound going.

You have begun to build your composition. Remember the image of the wall (see the drum roll for section 2, activity 3). Keep going until everyone in the group has joined in.

Then simply enjoy the amazing result. Close your eyes and really listen.

When you are ready let the group know you are going to finish with a gentle a… a… a… and STOP. If this is too intrusive, find your own way of finishing.

That's how to make the music, now for the bath! Invite someone to lie down in the middle of your circle so as to be surrounded entirely by your wonderful vocal music.

Begin your new composition all over again. Allow some silence at the end for the person 'in the bath' to come back to the real world. Ask him how it felt.

Why we like it

- ★ You don't need any instruments other than your voice
- ★ You begin to experiment with your voice alone, leaving words behind
- ★ Your confidence in using your voice grows
- ★ You feel amazed and empowered with the wonderful music that develops
- ★ You build your listening skills
- ★ You experience how important each person's contribution is and how it adds to the whole until this is much more than the sum of its parts!
- ★ You'll want to do it again and again

What next

You could conduct it in a simple way and enjoy the effect of getting louder or softer.

You might try using body percussion as well (see section 2, activity 13).

Once your composition is in full swing, keep going but quieten it down a little, then sing over the top the name of the person who is lying down in the middle. This is particularly helpful if the person in the 'bath' is a child or young person with profound and multiple learning difficulties.

Soundbite on the sound bath

A youthworker invented an adaptation of the sound bath, played on a resonance board, to explore risk with some young people. She made up a simple story about a young person going into a shop to steal something and then being seen and chased. One young person lay on the resonance board and imagined he was the character in the story. As the youthworker told the story, the other young people around the resonance board played rhythms to match the tension and adrenalin that would accompany such a scene. It was quite a gentle, slow, relaxed beat as the character wandered along the street wondering what to do. As he approached the shop, with the idea of stealing, the beat got a little stronger and faster. When the stealing was about to happen, the steady thump of a heartbeat dominated the playing. Then, as he was chased, it speeded up dramatically. Everyone had been caught up in the rush of emotion and the young person on the board felt exhausted by the tension. What ensued was a very powerful discussion about risk, adrenalin and the effect it has on the body, and some very positive ideas about alternatives to stealing!

Activity 5
Instant songs

CD track 22

Creating your own songs very quickly!

What you will need

★ Some ideas for familiar tunes to suggest
★ Big pieces of paper and pens

How to do it

Choose a tune that everyone knows – start with something really simple and easy to sing (nursery rhymes are good for this). Favourites of ours include 'London's Burning' and 'Frère Jacques'. Pick a theme, for example 'Food we like' or 'Food we don't like' or 'Things we like to do'. Then ask for suggestions of words that fit the theme and fit the tune. Work line-by-line, writing down as you go.

'London's Burning' on a 'Food we like' theme might come out like this:

> 'We like pizza, we like pizza,
> We like sausage, we like sausage,
> Ketchup, ketchup,
> Then some ice cream, then some ice cream!'

You take suggestions from around the group, then sing it all together – an instant song!

Why we like it

★ If you pick a tune everyone knows then no one has to worry about learning the tune
★ If you write the words down as you go along you really can sing it straight away
★ The song belongs to the group – it is very clear that they just wrote it!
★ You can pick themes relating to what you are doing: maybe your song is about a trip you've been on, or the best things about your playwork setting, or a member of staff who is leaving... the possibilities are endless.

What next?

Split into groups and write more songs: choose different tunes and different themes. Get groups to write their different versions of the same song and sing them in turn, and then all at the same time (very funny and chaotic but at least there is a definite end!). All write a version of 'London's Burning' and sing it in a round. Combine with other activities – see section 4.

Safety notes

With some groups you may wish to agree some ground rules on subject matter (especially if you split into small groups to write individual songs) just to be sure you don't end up with something very offensive or upsetting for anyone. On the other hand don't be afraid to use contentious themes – writing a song about something that makes you angry can be a very constructive way to confront it – just ensure that you protect vulnerable individuals. A song about how bad you think the local council is for closing your youth centre, or a rap about the local drugs scene could be deemed constructive. But a chant about what you think of Steve who stole your girlfriend might be less positive, especially for Steve!

Useful tips

Even if none of your group can read yet, write the words down so that you and any other playworkers can keep it going. You might want to draw little reminder pictures next to key words, but if children are used to learning songs without reading they will already have the skill – and of course, writing your own song makes it easier to remember!

For ideas on songs which make good starting points, see section 4, activity 4.

Soundbite on instant songs

A group of young people who belonged to a youth circus worked with one of their tutors to create a song about the circus to the tune of 'Doe a Deer' from the film 'The Sound of Music'. It was very catchy and soon the whole group knew the song. When they went to a national circus event with a parade through the streets of a major UK city, they began to sing their song and soon the whole crowd of circus performers was joining in!

If you're curious to know, it went like this (listen to the second part of the CD track number 22):

'The Sound of Circus'

Throw a ball, a juggling ball, toss a
diabolo up high,
Spin a plate, a spinning plate, you can
do it if you try.
Unicycle down the street,
Stilt walk on your little feet,
Tumble like an acrobat,
That will really make you throw,
throw, throw, throw,
Throw a ball... etc!

Activity 6
Calls and chants

CD tracks 23 to 38

Making calls and singing chants will bring a sense of empowerment and togetherness in your group. This activity helps to lift people's spirits, focus intention and build community

How to do it

If you have played the rhythm games in section 2 – where you call names or favourite foods, etc over the top of a basic beat – you have already been using calls and chants. Activity 6 introduces you to more formal chants which we have picked up over the years at various workshops, or when doing a 'chant swap' with friends.

Listen to the chants on the CD. Choose one you think your group will enjoy. Play it in the car or at home so it becomes familiar to you and you know it well. The better you know it the more comfortable you will be when you teach your group. As you teach it, show confidence in your voice, as this draws others in and builds enthusiasm. Encourage everyone to join in.

You may prefer to play the chant from the CD first to your group, then have a go at singing the chant with the CD. Once you all know it you can try without the CD.

You may want to add a basic beat on a drum, or begin with this and then sing the chant. Play around with it and above all have fun and enjoy chanting.

Some people may want to move or dance to the chant.

Why we like it

- ★ You don't need to learn a lot of words
- ★ The melodies are simple, so they are easy to learn and then repeat
- ★ You can add drums and percussion
- ★ There is no official ending – chants are continuous, so you can go on for as long as you want
- ★ You can adapt a chant very easily, writing your own words for specific occasions
- ★ You will find moving and dancing to them irresistible
- ★ They create different moods – loud and boisterous or quiet and meditative
- ★ Anyone can take the role of leading a chant

What next?

The football chant is a good way to bring a lively group together, giving them a sense of group empowerment without it ending like 'chaos on the terraces'. We are all familiar with the football rhythm-chant where we beat a rhythm and then call out our favourite football team at the end (see section 4, activity 2/CD track 42). Begin with one drum or piece of percussion and play the rhythm of the first part of the chant. Once you finish the rhythm bit, you call a person's name in the space at the end; then that person chooses a drum or percussion. Together you lead the chant again, playing the rhythm bit together and another person's name is called in the space. That person likewise chooses an instrument, and then the three of you lead the chant. Continue until you have a wonderful group rhythm-chant.

Soundbite on calls and chants

Once, in a music session with a group of young people with profound learning difficulties. we were doing a 'Pile up' (see section 2, activity 13) on one young woman's name. We were singing away, but it was hard to tell whether or not she was enjoying her personalised chant. So I made a call on top of the chant, calling out her name very high and stridently. The young woman lifted up her face, looked to where the call had come from and her face broke into a huge smile. Amidst the repetition of the chant the call had broken through and she knew something had happened: something different and pleasing; or maybe she just thought it was very funny.

We used the adapted football chant in the 'What next?' section above to introduce individuals at the beginning of a concert. Into each space created, a new person walked or ran onto the stage, stood still and shouted out his name. What a beginning!

Drum roll on calls

Calls are short melodic and verbal statements that convey information. They may tell someone to do something, announce someone or state a fact or intention.

Remember when you last called your cat or dog for their dinner, called the children in from the playground, called someone's name to attract his attention, or listened to your door bell?

How did you call? Do it again now. What does it sound like? What does your door bell sound like? Ask someone else to do the same. What do you notice about your calls?

You will probably find they are the same or very similar to track 23 on the CD. These calls are similar the world over.

Sometimes calls must penetrate other sounds and be capable of travelling over great distances: e.g. getting someone's attention over much noise or the Islamic call to prayer.

Calls can be used in musical activities to announce people, as in a welcome game or to announce a chant or game. They can be used to cut through other sounds to announce a chant or to change to another chant or rhythm game, especially for example, if you are processing in a carnival.

Drum roll on chants

Chants are a very ancient style of singing. They usually consist of only a few words and a simple melody. Often they take the form of a call and response where a call is made by the leader and the others in the group respond. The response is then repeated again and again, often over a rhythmic background, and becomes a chant.

Their purpose is to create particular mental and emotional states. They unify a group and create a feeling of power.

Do you remember chanting your times tables at school or chanting a slogan at a rally or football match? Or perhaps you have experienced chanting within a religious context, chanting prayers or a meditation.

What was it like to chant something over and over again? What was it like to do this with many other people? What effect did it have on the group?

We can use chants as a vehicle to express group support, to feel empowered, to help us become still and reflective. We can use chants in a robust way or in a more quiet way. Interestingly, once the chant is finished, silence follows, irrespective of whether it has been loud and boisterous or quiet and meditative: a silence that invites us in, that becomes a 'fruitful silence' (see the drum roll in section 2, activity 2).

Activity 7
Write a rap

CD tracks 39 and 40

A musical activity that encourages you to tell others about yourself and things important to you in a lively and fun way.

What you will need

★ Yourselves and your voices

How to do it

Rapping involves speaking about something – usually the ordinary and everyday things in life – in a rhythmic way over a strong basic beat. If you want to help a group to produce words for a rap, you can start by finding a theme they want to rap about.

Talk about the things that are important to them, or fun, or not so good, and decide which bits you want to include in a rap. Then look for key words in that theme and find other words that rhyme with them. For example, a rap some young people wrote about smoking began with a list of words: choking, joking, poking, stoking, no kin, Woking, yoking. The rap then formed around some of these words.

> 'The kids around here are all smokin',
> Pretty soon you know they gonna be
>   chokin'
> Cos the fire of death they are stokin'
> And you know that me I ain't jokin' '

The last word in a line tends to be the one emphasised, so good strong words here will get the ideas across.

Another way to set up a rap is to provide a vocal rhythm to underlie the rapping. You become a human beat box! You may find that some of the young people you work with can do this competently already. You use your mouth to make sounds like a drum machine, making a strong rhythm, which you keep going so that the rappers can do their stuff! You can have just one beat box, or a whole group keeping the rhythm. The rappers can prepare their words and then rap over the top. Listen to this on the CD track 39.

Why we like it

★ It's cool for any age group
★ Anyone can rap
★ Raps are easy to make up
★ You can inject your own personality into raps
★ You can rap about everything and anything
★ Raps are about the ordinary and everyday things in life so they can be used in any setting and for a multitude of purposes
★ You will want to move and keep that basic beat with finger clicks or body percussion

Useful tips

If working with teenagers you could begin by listening to the style of rap and hip-hop that they like. They will no doubt have already played around with the idea of raps and even made up their own. Tell them how rap came about (see drum roll on raps), especially the bit about how a DJ would make up rhymes about people attending a party. Use this as an idea to make a group rap about the people who come to your group. Raps are also a great way to sum up discussions you may have had around 'hot' issues and a powerful way to present to others information about yourselves, your group or needs in your community.

One thing to remember is that raps do not have to rhyme. You can just talk in rhythm over a basic beat and you are rapping. It's as simple as that.

Soundbite on raps

After a training day with teachers in a special school, one teacher told us later that she had used rapping about an activity to encourage a child to pass a ball to another during a PE session. This child had been racing around the room and any attempt to encourage him to sit with an adult and pass a ball met with huge resistance and struggle. So the teacher rapped what he had to do. He responded to the rhyme and repetition, and sat and passed the ball alongside an adult. The teacher used this rapping style successfully at other times during the day. She would sit alongside this little boy and rap about the activity he was doing – not worrying about it rhyming but simply saying aloud in a rhythmical way what he was doing. She observed him growing calmer, and he would sometimes smile and join in. She felt by rapping in this way she made a good connection with him about things that were important to him.

In the late eighties when rap was new to Europe, I was waiting for a train in Stuttgart, Germany, and heard a sound that was fresh, new and immediate. Two soldiers from a local military base were rapping. One of them was the human beat box, creating rhythms which resounded off the walls of the underground station, while the other improvised a rap over the top. It was instant, vibrant expression, which could not fail to capture the imagination of those listening. Rap, in its raw state, has great power.

A youthworker who in his spare time experimented with electronic music, added another dimension to a rap session when he recorded a backing rhythm for the young people to use. This meant that with very little preparation time they could get their ideas organised into words and then perform their own rap to their peers later that day, without the stress of having to keep the rhythm going too.

What next?

Try the body rap with your group: CD track 40. Words for the body rap can be found in Appendix 2. You can use photos of body parts to help people with communication difficulties select the body part they want to rap about.

Drum roll on raps

Rap is music created by African-American musicians. It is a form of expression whose roots are embedded deep within ancient African culture and oral tradition. Early forms were songs that had a melodic line and a strong rhythmic beat with repeated choruses. Throughout American history there has always been some form of verbal acrobatics or jousting involving rhymes within the African-American community: e.g. schoolyard rhymes, prison 'jail house' rhymes, jump-rope rhymes. These are some of the various forms of rap. Modern rap has its immediate roots in the dub talk over elements of reggae music. In the early days young partygoers initially recited popular phrases and used the slang of the day. It was popular for the DJ to acknowledge who was in attendance at a party, rapping a rhyme about them and evoking a response from the crowd. As this evolved, party shouts became more elaborate and it wasn't long before people began drawing on the outdated schoolyard rhymes. These were extended and customised to make them suitable for a party. Rap caught on because it offered young urban New Yorkers a chance to express themselves freely. More importantly, it was an art form accessible to everyone. Rap also became popular because it offered unlimited challenges. There were no real set rules, except to be original and to rhyme on time to the beat of music. Anything was possible. One could make up a rap about the man in the moon or how good a DJ was. The ultimate goal was to be seen as 'def' (good) by your peers. Finally, rap's inclusive aspects allowed people to inject their personality into it. If you were laid-back you could rap at a slow pace. If you were hyperactive you could rap at a fast pace. No two people rapped the same even when reciting the same rhyme. Break-dancers and graffiti artists provided a dramatic and colourful visual style to accompany the beats and narratives, and a subculture was born. This developed in the 80s and 90s into what we now call hip-hop.

Activity 8
Let's improvise!

CD track 41

Experimenting with vocal sounds and harmonies

What you will need

- ★ A group of singers – no more than 10
- ★ Confidence to experiment and make a noise

How to do it

Having warmed up your bodies and voices, stand in a circle and take a few deep breaths together. Relax. Anyone can start singing anything at any time. No sound is wrong or unacceptable. There are no rules. The key to successful improvisation is to listen to the sounds other people are making so that your sound can either complement theirs or take the improvisation in a new direction. If you want to agree a simple structure to get you started, you can simply sing notes on an 'ah' or 'ooh' sound. I call this 'angel voices', as you will find you can make beautiful, gentle, soothing harmonies.

As the group's confidence builds you can make rhythmic sounds, introduce little tunes, make spontaneous harmonies with others, hum, click, hiss. It can be fun to choose a theme and see what happens. You can have anything as a theme – time, light, chocolate, jazz, Africa, just a word like 'sparkle'; agree your theme and see where it takes you.

We have included an example of improvisation on the CD. There was no planning; the piece just developed according to what the group members felt inspired to sing. This may all sound very daunting, and it is certainly not an activity for beginners, or young children, but if you dare to give it a try we are confident you and those you sing with will be amazed at the beautiful music you can create.

Why we like it

- ★ Everyone participates, contributing whatever they feel comfortable to sing
- ★ This creates a safe space to experiment with the sounds you make
- ★ There is no pressure to sing the right note, every note is right in an improvisation
- ★ When you become absorbed by the music and your part in it you become very relaxed and can feel deeply refreshed
- ★ Improvisations only exist for those involved in them while they are being sung. This freedom to create can be very liberating
- ★ If you want to stop singing and listen for a while that is fine too
- ★ You can release a range of emotions by the way you choose to sing

What next?

You can improvise to give someone a sound bath (section 3, activity 4). You can improvise around someone on a resonance board.

Soundbite on improvisation

A group of young people who knew me and each other very well, and who had recently worked hard to put on a spectacular show, were on a residential weekend near the sea. They wanted to sing but they were tired of rehearsing to get their parts right. We had warmed up, played some games like 'Repeat after me' and done some chanting. It was a warm afternoon and we were outside. There was a gentle breeze and we could see the sea. We were all quite tired but still enjoying our singing workshop. I suggested we try 'Let's improvise!' With a little reassurance and a promise that anyone could take a 'sound bath' in the centre at any time, everyone agreed to give it a try. We spent at least half an hour singing, exploring, improvising, experimenting and creating beautiful sounds, just for ourselves, just for that moment. We were all on a natural high for the rest of the day!

Useful tips

It is OK to join in with someone else if you like what they are doing. They might then move on, or change slightly to add to what they have started. It's fine to do the same thing for a long time – often you get mesmerised by a rhythm and keep it going. This can be really inspiring to others who are free to improvise over your beat. It is OK to stop and listen until you feel ready to join in again.

Improvisations tend to come to a natural end. If you are the leader and you need to end the activity you can try slowing down the rhythm or making a gentle shhh sound to bring the volume down and encourage everyone to stop. Because you are all listening so intently this works very easily.

Section 4

Finding Ways to Bring Music into Other Activities

Activity 1
Sound effects

Combining music with story telling games

What you will need

- ⋆ A selection of noisemakers – musical instruments, instruments you have made, or found objects which make a noise (see section 1, activity 4)
- ⋆ Either a ready-made story: one from a book or one you made up earlier
- ⋆ Or be prepared to invent a story on the spot

How to do it

If your starting point is a ready-made story then first you need to look for possibilities within it for creating sound effects. Then match the noisemakers you have already to the sound effects you need for your story. For example, if you chose a fairy tale like 'The Three Little Pigs' you might have an instrument to make the sound of the pigs trotting along, another for the sound of straw, another for sticks and another for bricks. As you tell the story the noises are made at the appropriate moment. In this story you would also need a noise for the Big Bad Wolf – I'm sure the children would come up with a way to make the huffing and puffing sound! Decide on which sound is which and who will play each sound, then tell your story with sound effects.

If you are confident enough to make up a story on the spot this can be even more fun. A good way to start is with the noisemakers themselves. Play each one in turn and ask the group what they think each instrument could be a

sound effect for. Then you will have a series of elements around which to make up the story. For example, someone might have a bell and suggest it is the sound of fairy wings, a drum might be thunder, a shaker might be the rain, some blocks might be horses hooves… suddenly you have a starting point to build a story, and depending on the group you can either lead or ask for suggestions and let the children make up the story themselves.

Why we like it

- ★ It adds another dimension to story-telling
- ★ It is a way to use your instruments which does not involve any musical skill
- ★ It can build confidence around playing an instrument with or in front of other people
- ★ It can keep attention focused on a relatively calm activity

What next?

You can take your shared story-telling a step further by giving everyone an instrument and then telling the story around the circle, each person making up her own bit of the adventure, inspired by the noise maker she has and providing her own sound effects.

Useful tips

Although the above examples are aimed at younger children, this activity can work equally well with teenagers. Inventing adventure stories or soap opera-type yarns can be great fun and gives scope for more sophisticated sound effects. They can even retell a story they all know, such as a plot from a film they have all seen. Imagine the potential for sound effects in a ten minute re-telling of the 'Lord of the Rings' or the latest sci-fi horror movie!

Soundbite on sound effects

On a play-scheme the playleader really wanted to encourage some 'sitting down time' after a very physically active session. The group of children had made instruments earlier in the week and were delighted to play with them again… sitting down, attentive to the story, waiting for their turn to provide a sound effect (and, of course calming down and not running around for a while).

Activity 2
Supporters' club

CD track 42

Bringing music to sports activities

What you will need

* Instruments or voices or both!

How to do it

Be inspired by any sporting or team event and create your own musical way to support it. There are many ways to do this:

* Think stadium: have a band that parades around the pitch before the match begins
* Think American sports: cheerleaders with chants, actions and maybe even pom poms!
* Think football terraces: make up songs about your team or the event
* Think Olympics: have music to celebrate achievement
* Think New Zealand Rugby: get the team to devise their own vocal warm-up to match a physical one

Why we like it

* Sports events can often feel exclusive to many children – this is a creative way to get those not involved in sports to participate in the event and support those who are.
* It can make a group spectacle from a tournament that may have only involved a few players.
* The team playing can get a boost from the attention.
* It can add another dimension to the experience for the players (especially if they think that music is not their thing!)

Soundbite on supporters' club

The annual playscheme 5-a-side football tournament was loved by the keen players but was annoying and intrusive for everyone else. The event was transformed when each team had its own chant and everyone learned the 5-a-side football song that a small group of children composed one day. Everyone enjoyed and, more importantly, felt part of the final as the 'band' (children who had made instruments and played lots of music games during the weeks of the playscheme) marched around the pitch playing before the match. Songs were sung, chants were chanted, and the band played again when all the players in the competition received their applause.

Safety notes

If you are making up songs (see section 3, activity 5) and are using the theme of football terraces, you need to agree some ground rules about permissible language and keeping the songs positive. Football chants are not renowned for being polite and inoffensive!

Useful tip

Allow your imagination to include any sporting event. You could invent some great songs or chants about pool, darts, swimming, running races, rounders… the possibilities are endless!

Drum roll on using sport to inspire music making

Supporters' club can get non-sporty types to participate in sporting events by using music. You can also use it to get sporty types into playing music!

Use the rhythm of the well-known football chant… Da da … da da da … da da da da … ENGLAND! as a starting point for a name game (as on the CD track 42). All beat the rhythm together and leave the space at the end for someone to call out their name. You might even get them performing! We worked for several weeks with a youth group for young people with learning difficulties, and they decided to put together a performance for their parents. As their 'opening number' they were all off stage and one person began the football rhythm on a drum. While this was happening the first person ran onto the stage and in the space usually reserved for calling a football team she stopped, lifted up her arms and shouted out her name. People performed in different, invented styles, and this was a great way to introduce everyone in the performance individually.

Activity 3
Beginners' opera

CD track 43

Combining singing and drama

What you will need

- ★ Confidence building for singing
- ★ Practice at inventing songs
- ★ Experience at improvising and acting out stories
- ★ A way to record your improvisation (pen and paper, tape recorder, video camera)

How to do it

Explain that in opera no one speaks, everyone sings to tell the story and communicate with each other. If you use drama games with your group, they will be used to acting out stories, either inventing the plot in advance, or improvising as they go along. For this game they will only be allowed to communicate by singing. It does not have to be a recognisable tune, just any tune for the words they want to say. To start with there is no need to consider rhyme and rhythm, just sing what you would normally say. Once

participants have got the hang of this they can try to make their sentences rhyme or make the rhythm of their line match the rhythm of the line before.

Eg.
'I want to go to town'
'You know I hate to shop'
'I want to go right now'
'I wish that you would stop'

Once you get started this can be infectious and very funny! It is often hard to stop once you've got into it!

Why we like it

- ★ It can add another dimension to drama activities
- ★ It is fun and funny
- ★ It can seem impossible to start with, then it usually gets easier and so is a rewarding process

What next?

Your opera can be purely an improvisation that exists only while it is being sung and enjoyed by those participating. That really is OK! However you can take it further by recording your efforts and working on them, refining the lyrics and coordinating the action. If you get really into it you can make a set and costumes and perform to your peers, or even a wider audience.

Useful tip

If you want to repeat the opera you have invented, you need to have a good way to record it, otherwise it is impossible to remember the lyrics and tunes. Probably the best way is to record it all on video. Otherwise you can tape it. As a last resort write it down as you go along but it really is much easier to write down from a recording that you can stop and start.

Soundbite on beginner's opera

A youth group were exploring issues relating to bullying and hoping to devise some anti-bullying strategies. After an intense discussion which raised some very sensitive issues, they created a beginners' opera which depicted scenes where bullying behaviour was taking place and a 'bullying-busting' superhero would intervene. It was hilarious and far-fetched, of course, but the follow-up work they did threw up some excellent anti-bullying strategies, many of which were workable solutions inspired by the over-the-top antics of their operatic superhero!

Activity 4
Puppet musical

Bringing music to stories told with puppets

What you will need

- ★ Puppets! Either professionally made ones or puppets made by the children
- ★ Ideas about characters
- ★ A story
- ★ Some songs you all know

How to do it

Gather your puppets! Ask each child to bring her puppet if she has made one, or choose a puppet if you are using ready-made ones and play with it: find out how it moves, what it can do, get to know it. Then ask each child to name her puppet and find out something else about it by asking another question, such as 'What is your puppet's favourite food?' or 'Tell me something that your puppet once did that was a bit naughty' or 'What does your puppet like to do best?' Write all these ideas down and then move on to something else. Give yourself some time to think about a story that incorporates all the puppet characters. (We usually do this over lunchtime, or even overnight, ready for the next session). Your story is likely to be a bit contrived, but the characteristics the children suggested can give inspiration. The question about 'something naughty' often gives great plot material. One of the exciting things is that each puppet gets a mention.

Your next challenge is to set up the puppet show. We always play this with at least two playworkers: one gets a group of children to make a set or backdrop for the puppet show and the other works with other children on devising the songs. All you do is find points in the story that can be illustrated by a song and play 'instant songs' (section 3, activity 5), creating some words about your story to familiar tunes. The songs can be used to introduce characters or tell parts of the story.

Here's an example from a pirate story, at the point the pirates are introduced to the audience – sung to the tune of the Grand Old Duke of York:

> 'Oh! Pirates are so bad, they like to
> roam the seas,
> They capture people, chop them up
> and eat them for their tea!'

You don't need many songs, but it is particularly good if you have an ending number.

The pirate story above (after some adventures with mermaids and Triton!) ended with a song to celebrate a happy outcome – sung to the tune of London's Burning:

> 'We're the pirates, we're the pirates
> But we're good now, but we're good
> now
> We'll protect you, we'll protect you
> As long as we live'

Once you have a few songs, write the words on big pieces of paper (flip chart, or old wall paper) then gather your cast. Get them behind the set and begin to narrate the story so that the puppets can pop up when it is their moment.

When it is time for a song, hold up the words, tell everyone the tune and – Hey Presto! – you can all sing the songs straight away!

End with a rousing tune that allows all the puppets to dance about together, and you have created your very own puppet musical.

Why we like it

- ★ It gives a focus to puppet-making activities
- ★ The show is a great buzz for everyone involved
- ★ It can be surprisingly spectacular with the combination of puppets, set and songs
- ★ It is a way to work with a smaller number of enthusiastic children on a project which they can perform to their peers
- ★ The children who make the puppets do not have to be the ones who make the set and create the songs.
- ★ The audience becomes involved too because they sing all the songs

Useful tips

We usually keep the set-making playworker backstage to supervise the performers, and the song-making playworker takes the narrator role.

Although we advocate empowering children, the narrator role is crucial for holding everything together, directing the action and the music too. We suggest therefore that you take this role! In fact it seems unfair to put that much pressure on a child at play!

Tunes we have found to be good starting points

- ★ Happy Birthday to you (great for endings – people are used to singing it with gusto!)
- ★ London Bridge is Falling Down (potential for lots of verses and the repeats make it easier to learn)
- ★ TV themes like Postman Pat and Eastenders
- ★ Teddy Bears Picnic
- ★ The Grand Old Duke of York
- ★ Row, Row, Row your Boat (another good one for multiple verses)
- ★ Frère Jaques
- ★ Here Comes the Bride
- ★ We wish you a Merry Christmas
- ★ Any current, catchy pop tune, particularly 'naff' ones!

Soundbite on puppet musical

Although the above examples refer to children, this activity works equally well with adolescents. I would not suggest devising the story with a group of twenty 6 – 10-year-olds, but a group of teenagers could write their own story based on puppet characters. Puppets may at first seem childish but it doesn't take long to find adult puppets such as animatronics characters in movies, large parade structures, (examples in the book 'Engineers of the Imagination' – details in Bibliography, Sources and Useful Addresses) and old TV shows like 'Spitting Image'. An older child's creation can be more high tech or just BIG to make them feel more challenging. One group of teenagers made themselves into puppets, by making costumes and painting features onto their bodies with face paint. One boy made a huge hat which covered his face and shoulders, then he painted a face onto his chest with his belly button as the mouth and his legs became the puppet's body. Another made a giant puppet built on a rucksack frame. Their story had a strong youth angst feel about it and all the music was rap, except for a rather moving ballad based on a current pop hit, sung by two of the girls.

Drum roll on inventing characters

Be prepared for gory and even violent ideas. They are not inevitable but more often than not at least a few of the characters are 'evil' just as in cartoons and stories. Don't get hung up on this or feel you have to keep your story 'nice'. Dragons which eat people, aliens intent on murder, children who steal can all be worked into an intriguing story with a positive end. It is important not to censor children's ideas unless they are really offensive to others.

Activity 5
Musical cascade

Harnessing the music enthusiasm of a group of children to create a performance where everyone gets to take part

What you will need

- ★ A group of children or young people who have played lots of the games in section 2 and 3 and who would like to do a show for their peers
- ★ All the other children, young people and adults in your setting (or even an invited audience)
- ★ Instruments for all the performers
- ★ If you want to, you can provide your audience with instruments; or it's fine to get them to use their bodies (clap, stamp, slap thighs etc)
- ★ An area for the 'stage' and an area for the 'auditorium'!

How to do it

This activity can range from being a very short piece of 'sharing' by one group to another, through to being a longer, more elaborate show.

You can use many of the rhythm games in section 2 to instantly involve an audience. You could teach them all to keep a basic beat and then the performers can 'show off' over the top of it by building a 'Pile up' (section 2, activity 14). Anyone who really wants to shine could have a turn at 'Walking on the wall' (section 2, activity 16). You could divide your audience into sections and get them to join you in 'Foodies' (section 2, activity 6), teaming up different performers with each section. It is crucial to teach your audience the 'Stop-start game' (section 2, activity 1) and then you could have a giant rumble (section 2, activity 2). How about getting them all on their feet and 'Legging it' (section 2, activity 3)? Don't forget 'Orchestration' (section 2, activity 15) and the potentially empowering feeling of controlling everyone in the room! For a similar impact, some of your performers could take it in turns to be callers for 'Copy me do' (section 2, activity 10).

Then, of course, you can use games from section 3 for audience participation. You can all have fun warming up your bodies and voices, get them to respond to your calls in 'Repeat after me' or even teach them one of your instant songs. An audience could provide a beat for a rap or you could work in a part where everyone joins in – there could be a line that repeats at the end of each verse, for example, or a sound like 'Huh' to join in with every so often when you give the signal. You could even teach them a group chant.

If you are looking for an exciting finale turn to the next section – all of the 'finding an end' activities could be adapted to work in a setting with an audience.

Why we like it

★ It can provide a focus for the end of a series of music sessions
★ It is a way to make a show from activities which are essentially about participation, not about performance
★ It is a way to be part of a music performance without having to be an experienced and traditionally talented musician
★ The scope for children and young people to lead is plentiful – this can be fantastic for building self-esteem, and gaining the respect of others
★ The enthusiasm of the performers can inspire others who were not so keen to join in music activities
★ It can form part of a larger show with a variety of activities which have taken place in your setting
★ It makes a wonderful end to a playscheme, term or project – music can really bring people together and leave you all feeling exhilarated!

Useful tips

To make this work you must teach the audience the Stop-start game (section 2, activity 1). You, or whoever is leading, needs that control!

Depending on the size of your audience compared to the size and volume of your band, you might need to experiment with different levels of sound if they provide a backing beat. If clapping and stamping are simply too loud, try gently slapping thighs, clicking fingers or brushing the palms of the hands together.

Make sure you include a chance for the performers to thank the audience, as well as for the performers to receive their appreciation.

Activity 6
Music on the move

CD tracks 44 and 45

Using music to create a carnival

What you will need

★ Lots of loud percussion instruments (home-made or bought)
★ Songs, chants and rhythms you have all practised
★ Costumes
★ Flags, puppets or anything else you can think of!

How to do it

You can use your musical instruments to make a parade come to life. Once you have mastered 'Legging it' you can branch out into walking and playing!

If you use a simple call and response rhythm combined with the basic beat, you have the beginnings of a Samba band. Listen to CD track 44 to hear how you can start off your basic beat and layer a simple '1 2 3' call over it, to which you respond with another rhythm. As in 'Foodies', words can help with keeping the rhythm, or can even become a chant. We have used: '1 2 3' – 'What are we here for?' and on a playscheme in a local community in Swansea called Blaen-y-maes, the call became 'Blaen-y-maes' – 'We're on the playscheme' and a group of young people at a children's rights event came up with 'Children's Rights' – 'You have to listen!'. Over this last rhythm some of the group sang 'We want our rights and we want them now'. Listen to CD track 44 to see how it all fits together.

If this all sounds too complicated for you at the moment, you can keep it even simpler by using the following games from section 2: 'Copy me do', 'Number one to number five' and 'All about eight'.

Another effective rhythm for a parade is 'Eight train'. (CD track 45). You just count to eight over and over again, and each time play one more of the beats. So for the first round everyone hits their drums or shakes their shakers once on the first beat, then quietly counts '2 3 4 5 6 7 8'; then they play 2 beats and quietly count '3 4 5 6 7 8'; then 3 beats and count '4 5 6 7 8' – and so on, until all eight beats are played. The next round you go back to playing just one beat again and repeat the sequence as many times as you like. This creates a very dramatic sound. Someone once suggested that it sounds like a train approaching!

Of course familiarity with 'a…a…a… and stop' is vital for your parade and as long as you can make yourself heard you could do 'Rumbles' or even a 'Pile up' as you go along (see section 2).

As for singing and chanting, this can be combined with the instruments, or you can incorporate chants into your parade. If you

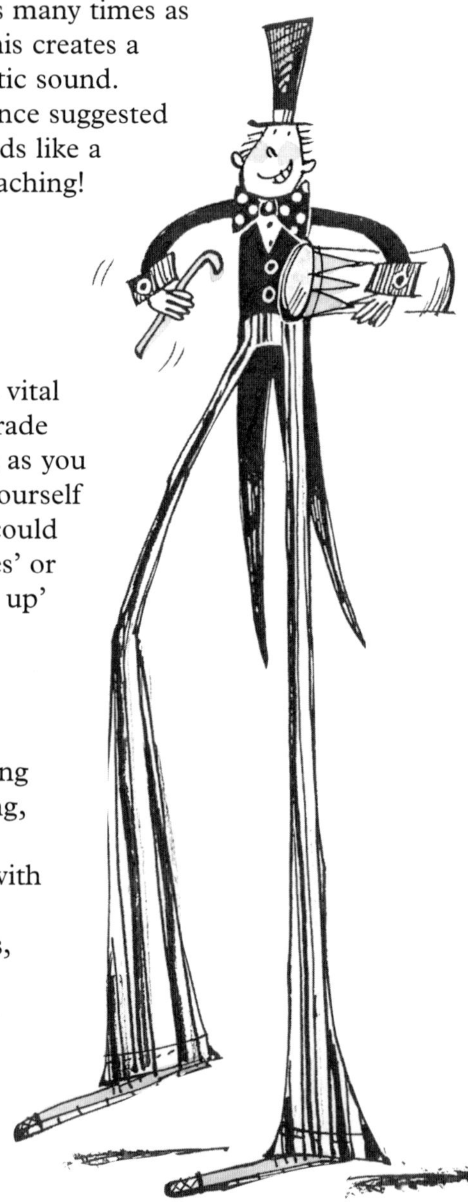

have some strong and confident volunteers you can play 'Repeat after me' (section 3) on the move. It works especially well if the leaders prepare their calls in advance and repeat them, so people know roughly what's coming. Write your own instant songs and all learn them before you set off.

Why we like it

★ It can be really exciting to take your music out into the world!
★ You can use a carnival to publicise an event or raise awareness of your project
★ It is rewarding to take your new skills a step further
★ Leading a chant or rhythm game on a carnival is great for building confidence
★ It's a legitimate reason to make a big noise in the street!

Safety notes

You can, of course, parade inside around your venue, but if you are venturing outside you need to walk the route beforehand and check that it is safe and suitable for your group. If you do make any banners or other large decorations, check they won't get tangled in wires or doorways.

What next?

Your parade can be just about the music but, if you want to create a real carnival atmosphere, why not make costumes or banners? Hats, headdresses, scarves tied around wrists, tabards, face paint… get your group to use their imaginations! You can even make giant puppets (see section 6 for info on books for inspiration) or impressively tall decorations by decorating a hula-hoop with bits of fabric and securing the hoop to the top of a long bamboo pole. Dressing-up can add so much to the effect.

Soundbite on Music on the move

At a week-long international jamboree for Guides and Scouts we ran a drop-in area where young people came to make scrap instruments, play rhythm games, make up chants, design and produce banners and create giant puppets. On the final evening of the event, 50 or so young people gathered to make a carnival parade. Some held banners, some operated giant puppets, some played instruments and they all made music! We played 'Eight train' to get the attention of the thousands of other people in the surrounding fields and then led the way to the closing ceremony with a combination of simple samba, the basic beat, and chants we had devised during the week. We ended up on the stage, getting everyone assembled to join in with some call and response ('Repeat after me') and singing our chant; and then ended it all with a giant 'Rumble', which was met with tremendous applause. Everyone agreed this was a spectacular way to celebrate the end of an amazing week.

Drum roll on carnival traditions

Most people are aware of the carnivals of Brazil, Notting Hill and the

Caribbean. The tradition began hundreds of years ago in Europe when Catholics in Italy began to hold wild costume festivals on the eve of Lent. Because they did not eat meat during Lent, the festival was known as 'carnevale' which translates as 'farewell to meat'. The tradition spread to other Catholic countries in Europe and so when, in the 18th Century, countries such as Spain, France and Portugal began to colonise other parts of the world, they took their tradition with them. African slaves taken to these colonies brought their own traditions with them, which were adopted into the carnival celebrations – parading, drumming, using natural objects like feathers, making giant sculptures, stilt walking. In Trinidad carnival arrived with the French settlers in the 18th century but only in 1834, when slavery was abolished and the emancipated slaves took to the streets to celebrate their new freedom, did it become a giant singing, dancing street party!

Today carnival continues to be an exciting way to celebrate and bring people together.

Section 5

Finding an End

Activity 1
Zuma chant

CD track 46

A chant to bring a strong and rousing end to any session or conference.

How to do it

This chant has 6 vocal layers to it – and yes, you can do it! Listen to the chant on the CD to hear it chanted altogether and then to hear each of the parts separately, and how they 'pile up' on top of each other. As you listen, follow the layers below.

Then teach the chant to your group, one layer at a time. It is best to space it out over a few weeks and make sure they know one or two layers really well before learning the next layer to put on top.

Foundation layer A good, strong, basic beat on a drum

1 2 3 4 1 2 3 4 etc.

Layer 1

1	2	3	4
Zuma -	Zuma -	Zuma -	Zuma hey!

Layer 2

1	2	3	4
Zuma hey	Zuma -	Zuma ho	Zuma -

Layer 3 This is exactly the same as layer 2 only it begins one beat after layer 3

(1)	1	2	3	4
(layer 2)	Zuma hey	Zuma -	Zuma ho	Zuma -

Layer 4

1	2	3	4
Zuma laba	Zuma laba	Zuma laba	hey! hey!

Layer 5 This begins just before the first beat

-	1	2	3	4
Africa	Hey hey	Hey hey-ey	Zuma laba -	

Layer 6

1	2	3	4
A - fri -	ca hey	Zuma laba -	

Always make sure you have a strong basic beat to start it all off.

One fun way to stop is to get each layer in turn to change their call to 'Hey! Hey! Hey! Hey!' until everyone is chanting hey together. Then get louder and faster on the 'Heys'! and finish on one big HEY!

Why we like it

- ★ It is energetic, rousing and fantastic fun
- ★ It really helps to bring a group together
- ★ You will be able to chant a chant with 6 layers!
- ★ You can put percussion and drums with it so there is room for all tastes and level of skill

What next?

Whenever you chant 'Hey!' a really fun thing to do is to punch one arm into the air with a closed fist (a really strong warrior style movement). So at the end of layer 4 for example, you punch your arm and fist into the air twice for 'Hey! Hey!' When you chant 'ho', punch your arm down towards the ground.

One last challenge, try walking round the room chanting and using your arm movements at the same time.

I bet you perform this one many, many times.

Useful tip

If you do get people walking round the room while chanting Zuma (see soundbite) you will find they

automatically walk in a circle. It then gets very crowded and the effect is lost. So just remind people to use the whole space, walking across the circle, or on a diagonal etc.

Soundbite on Zuma

At the end of a music conference in Southampton we were asked if we could end the day with everyone joining in a chant. Well, needless to say, we chose Zuma! There were 150 people! We sang through each layer so people could hear them and choose which one they wanted to sing. Some layers appeal to those who want to sing low, some in the middle and some high. Then everyone went and stood in a big circle in order of vocal layers 1 through 6 and off we went. Once the layers had been piled up and the chant was gaining momentum we asked everyone to walk anywhere in the room, across the circle, diagonally or round the circle, and keep singing and punching the air on 'Hey!' What an amazing experience. Not only were you able to hear all the other layers as they 'walked by' you, but seeing arms going up all over the place and at different times was incredible. I stood on a chair – what a brilliant sight – to conduct the ending. We ended as explained above ('How to do it') with everyone shouting out 'Hey! hey! hey! hey!' – getting faster and faster, and then calling a… a… a… and STOP.

Activity 2
Lullabies

CD tracks 47 to 50

A way to bring quiet and relaxation into your group, and a peaceful way to end a music session.

What you will need

- ⋆ CD player
- ⋆ Jabulani CD
- ⋆ Space to lie down

How to do it

Listen to the lullaby, track 47 on the CD, and familiarise yourself with the very simple rhythm, tune and harmony. To begin with you may like to play the lullaby from the CD and just let people listen to it and relax at the end of your music session.

When you teach it to them make sure everyone is sitting or lying comfortably. Ask them to feel their heartbeat, either by placing their hand over their heart or feeling for their pulse in their neck or wrist. Try calling out the 'thub dub' of your heartbeat (see Drum roll in section 2, activity 10). Then play this rhythm quietly on a drum or your knees.

Begin to sing the lullaby and ask people to join in as they learn it. Once everyone is singing you can sing the harmony on top. Keep it going for many rounds, you will be able to judge when it is time to end it. About 4 rounds before the end instruct people to sing each round more and more quietly and gradually fade out.

Why we like it

- ★ It is so simple – one word and two notes
- ★ You can harmonise very simply on top of the basic tune
- ★ It makes people feel calm and relaxed
- ★ You can sing it as a group
- ★ You can sing it just with one child – a lovely, close time together
- ★ It is a peaceful way to end a session

Useful tip

This little chant is very powerful and people can be moved to tears. If this happens to someone in your group, don't be frightened by this. If you know the person well you may know why and may know whether to comfort him or let him be. If you don't know him very well just ask gently if he is alright, and if he would like you to sit with him for a bit.

What next?

Listen again to the lullaby on the CD – track 47. Try singing with the top part. Now split your group and have one half sing the basic tune and the other sing the harmony. You will be amazed at how simple but effective this is.

Soundbite on lullabies

One very, very hot summer we were working at a MENCAP play scheme. Having made music with small groups during the day, we were asked to end the day with a big finale. When all the children and young people and staff (about 80 in all) came into the huge sports hall, we could see how restless and hot and noisy everyone was. We decided to change plans and chose not to do a rousing chant but sing the lullaby over and over again instead, and just see what happened. Well at first we couldn't even hear ourselves over the noise and then gradually the noise level fell; and after 15 minutes (yes lullabies are meant to be sung for that long at least) you could hear a pin drop in the hall. One young woman was crying – the lullaby had touched a place inside her – she said she was not unhappy, just very moved. Time and again we have experienced the power of this little lullaby chant.

Drum roll on lullabies

Lullabies are unaccompanied songs or refrains to quiet children and lull them to sleep. The word 'lullaby' comes from putting the word 'lull' (which means to soothe or calm) together with the word 'by', as in goodbye. Virtually all cultural groups have lullabies, which are often passed on orally from one generation of parents to another. Lullaby lyrics can be nonsensical and repetitive. The words themselves do not always seem to be important, as they can tell about something else entirely or even frightening. Rather, it is the feeling and atmosphere that the simple, repetitive and smooth melodies provoke that makes a lullaby.

The rhythm of lullabies fits in with the 'thub dub' of our heartbeat in a 1 2 3 time, as opposed to a strong marching beat which has a 1 2 3 4 rhythm e.g.

Thub	dub	–	Thub	dub	–
1	2	3	1	2	3

Lullabies are often the first songs we remember from childhood and act as a link between generations. In Africa the women have to work very hard. They have to have their babies with them while they work, so often carry them on their backs. They keep moving and singing while they work in order to keep the baby asleep. Lullabies were often sung over the top of women's chatter and work. Much could be going on and still the baby would sleep – such is the power of the lullaby.

Lullabies may offer children, young people and adults a chance to find that quiet place that we may have missed out on for many reasons earlier in our lives.

If you are interested in knowing more about lullabies there is an excellent radio 3 website – www.bbc.co.uk/radio3/world/onyourstreet/chlullaby1.shtm where you can listen to lullabies from around the world.

Activity 3
Applaudian chair

A game to give everyone a chance to receive applause

What you will need

⋆ A chair

How to do it

Place the chair where everyone can see it and explain it is no ordinary chair but an applaudian chair. Then explain how it works: if anyone sits on the chair (or even places their hand on it) all the other people in the room begin to applaud them enthusiastically. Cheering and the Umfulosi Ulu (see below) are fine too! Then you need to test it. Carefully sit down and see if the applause begins. If it doesn't, pretend it's not switched on, find an imaginary switch at the back and try again. If the applause is a bit quiet then invent a volume switch and turn it up. All sound should stop the moment you stand up – remember it's the chair providing the signal! Once you are sure that the chair is 'working' you invite anyone who would like to, to sit on it.

Why we like it

⋆ It is a very effective way to offer praise to everyone
⋆ It is less intimidating than taking a bow
⋆ The applause only continues for as long as you are sitting on the chair, so you control how long it lasts

- ★ You get an enthusiastic response whoever you are and whatever you have achieved that day – how often in life can we guarantee that?
- ★ You can use it in a show and place something on the chair like a shoe and say 'this shoe represents all the audience', so they get some appreciation too.

Safety notes

Sometimes children want to stand on the chair – keep them safe if they do

Useful tips

You might need to gently encourage some people to sit on the chair. If they feel very shy, tell them the chair works just as well with two people on it so they can come up with their friends. Groups can all place a hand on. The chair has been known to travel to people for whom the very public move towards the chair is too intimidating. It can also pass its power to other chairs, which is particularly useful if you have any participants who use wheelchairs and are unable to transfer to the chair. However, never assume that a child using a wheelchair wants to receive their applause this way – help them make the transfer if they want to – they might just have picked up on the buzz you get from the real thing!

Soundbite on applaudian chair

Children on a playscheme loved this idea so much that they used it at the end of every week. They decorated the chair with fabric, tinsel and balloons so it looked really special.

Drum roll on giving applause

Applause will occur spontaneously in music sessions but sometimes you need a way to show your appreciation that doesn't involve your hands – especially if you are drumming! An alternative is to teach everyone the 'Umfolosi Ulu.'

Black Umfolosi are a performance group from Zimbabwe who teach this at their concerts to help Europeans relax and express themselves differently! If you are male you place your tongue behind your teeth and blow air through as if you were purring, then 'ooh' through it. If you are female you sing 'ooh' tapping your hand on your lips (like a Native American war cry!) Listen to the CD track 16 for a demonstration! And of course you don't have to be strict about the male/female sounds!

Drum roll on receiving applause

Not everyone is comfortable receiving praise. There can be many reasons for this: a person may be used to receiving a negative rather than a positive response to his actions. Music offers everyone the chance to become positively involved in something which inspires praise and respect from others. Make sure you create opportunities to recognise everyone's participation and achievements. If you do this in a non-intimidating way, using techniques such as the Umfolosi Ulu or applaudian chair, this can have a profound impact on an individual's self-esteem and foster a liking for this kind of positive, rather than negative response.

Activity 4
Rainstorm

CD track 51

A group activity which peaks in volume and returns to a calm and peaceful end

What you will need

★ Everyone sitting in a circle (on the floor or on chairs)

How to do it

Explain that you will keep moving around the circle doing different actions to make different sounds, and that when you are in front of a person (and not before!) he should change his action to match yours. Set the scene by telling the group that together they are going to create the sound of a rainstorm. As well as doing the actions they should listen to the overall sound the group is making. The following list is the sequence of actions – go round the circle completely before you start the next action.

1. rub your hands together
2. click your fingers
3. tap two fingers onto the opposite hand
4. clap
5. slap your thighs
6. beat the floor with your fists (or stamp your feet if you are sitting on chairs). This is the peak of the storm, and from here on it gets quieter.
7. slap your thighs

8. clap
9. tap your fingers more slowly
10. click fingers slowly
11. rub your hands together
12. put your finger to your lips to indicate no more sound

Why we like it

★ Rainstorm works because everyone plays their part
★ It sounds spectacular
★ It is very simple to set up
★ It takes the group to a climax of chaotic sound before bringing it back down to a peaceful end
★ There is always a sense of calm after the storm which can ease the passage from a music session to another activity

Useful tips

You may need to adapt the sequence of actions to include all your participants. If some can't click, leave out the clicking and just open and close your hands quickly instead; if some can't clap, provide an alternative which all can manage.

Safety notes

It can be quite tiring to move around the circle 12 times if you have a large group. Be kind to yourself! One solution is to just turn on the spot, making eye contact with each person as you go round. Alternatively, particularly with older children, you can sit as part of the circle and ask the person on your left to copy you, the person on his left to copy him, and so on round the circle, a bit like a 'Pile up' (section 2, activity 13). When you see that everyone is doing the first action you start the second, which gets passed on in turn – and so on. This takes concentration and a bit of discipline for everyone to wait for 'their' moment before changing sounds, so we find it easier to do the 'moving around' version and see the more self-directed form as the intermediate stage. You can play 'advanced' rainstorm when you are so focused that you can pass the changes around with your eyes shut. Very satisfying!

What next?

Try playing rainstorm on a resonance board. It is a wonderful experience.

If you play parachute games this works well inside a parachute tent, especially when it's hot!

A nice end to a rainstorm is to get everyone to stretch their arms up towards the ceiling and then bring them back down to their sides (as though drawing a semi-circle in the air). You all do this together and it symbolises the sun coming out!

Activity 5
Sound feedback

Noise-based evaluation technique

What you will need

★ Some evaluation questions
★ You can use instruments if you have them to hand

How to do it

Ask a question and tell the group to respond to it by making a sound corresponding to their answer. So if their response was 'Yes, great, fantastic' they would make as much noise as they could. If it was 'OK, fine, not too bad' they would make less noise. If it was 'No, rubbish, boring, wish I'd stayed at home' then they make little or no noise.

You ask questions such as:

★ 'Have you tried something new today?'
★ 'Did you make a noise today?'
★ 'Would you like to do this again?'
★ 'Have you had fun?'

and gauge the answer by the volume and enthusiasm of response you hear!

Why we like it

★ You can end the session with even more noise
★ Evaluation questions give everyone a chance to reflect on their experience
★ You can comment on their response by giving more information – a loud response to 'Would you like to this again?' would leave you space to advertise the next session.

Useful tip

You can monitor the responses with a 'noiseometer'. Place your hands palms together with the back of one hand pointing towards your knee. As the noise increases lift the other hand accordingly – the louder the noise the further apart you move your hands.

You can also record it if you want to by drawing a scale or ruler on a large piece of paper and marking how high up the ruler the sound goes.

bash bash
clunck
clunck
Ding ding
bash
bash
rattle
rattle
boom
boom

aaaah
oooooooohh
aaaaah
ooooh
mmmm

Appendix 1

Sample Programmes

If you are new to running music sessions and are wondering where to start, the following programmes are tried and tested combinations of activities. We have given each programme a title to give you some idea of the way we would use and structure these sessions – but do feel free to adapt and change them to suit you and your group.

Half-hour to 45-minute session for younger children

Activities

1. Begin with the 'Stop-start' game (section 2, activity 1), just using slapping knees or stamping feet or running on the spot, or shaking arms etc to begin with. Play it many times and let one or two children have a go at leading the stop.
2. Then try a chant from section 3, activity 6. Listen to the CD. Choose one that creates a space into which children can put their names. 'Hi Ya Ma' would be a good one to begin with.
3. Still using voices try 'Repeat after me' (section 3, activity 3). With young children it is best for you to be the only person making the basic beat on a drum or strong percussion instrument. Children can use their hands on their knees.
4. Then bring out some percussion and drums and combine the 'Stop-start' game with the 'Rumbles'. Play it many times, again with some children leading the Stop and maybe even the Start.
5. Introduce 'Beat, beat, beat upon the tom-tom!' (section 2, activity 11) by listening to it on the CD and moving to it and chanting it. You can develop it in the next session.
6. Then choose one more activity from section 2 that appeals to you – perhaps 'Vanessa's game' (section 2, activity 5) or 'Copy me do' (section 2, activity 10) or 'Foodies' (section 2, activity 6).
7. Finish your session either with a rousing chant with percussion accompaniment e.g. 'Tongoya' (CD track 31) or a lullaby (CD Tracks 47, 48, 49 and 50).

One to one-and-a-half hour session for older children and young people

Activities

1. Begin with 'Legging it' (no. 2 of the 'Basic beat' game (section 2, activity 3). Enjoy the rap that accompanies this activity.
2. Keep going with this game and try putting the claps, calls or body actions on top (see 'What next?' under 'Legging it'). Finish it all with the 'Stop-start' game (section 2, activity 1).
3. While you are all standing go on to 'Rhythm whispers' (section 2, activity 12).
4. Time for a chant – Choose one that has spaces in it where the people in your group can insert their names, or where they are from, or favourite pop groups etc. Some of these are Helele

Mama, (CD track 26) Jabulani (CD track 24) Hi Ya Ma (CD track 25) or Tongoya (CD track 31).

5. Play another rhythm game, 'Number one to number 5' (section 2, activity 9) using claps to keep the basic beat.
6. New chant – you may want to use this slot in your session to teach a new chant over several sessions. Choose one from section 3 activity 6 (CD tracks 24 to 38).
7. Drum and Percussion time:
   a. 'Rumbles' combined with the 'Stop-start' game
   b. 'Copy me do'
   c. 'Pile up'
   d. 'Orchestration'.
8. You can choose the type of finish you want:
   Rousing – 'Zuma' chant (section 5, activity 1 – CD track 46)
   Calming – A lullaby (section 5, activity 2 – CD tracks 47, 48, 49 and 50)
   Percussion – 'Rainstorm' game (section 5, activity 4 – CD track 51).

A session with no instruments

One of the great things about music is that you can have a great session without any instruments, equipment or materials (and once you are familiar with the games and chants, you won't need much preparation time either!)

Activities

1. Start with 'Warm up your body' (section 3, activity 1).
2. Then 'Warm up your voice' (section 3, activity 2). Don't forget you can use the CD to lead these warm ups until you feel ready to lead them yourself (but you need a CD player of course!).
3. Play 'Legging it' (section 2, activity 3) to help everyone feel the basic beat.
4. Keep 'legging it' as you play 'Repeat after me' (section 2, activity 3).
5. Then move on to a chant like 'Vi vo vista' or 'Ungawa' (CD tracks 20 and 27). They are call and response chants so you can lead into them nicely from the previous game.
6. Have a break from singing and hone your rhythm skills – play 'Rhythm whispers' (section 2, activity 12).
7. Sit in a circle and play 'Vanessa's game'.
8. Choose another chant or two. Maybe the group is ready for the challenge of a round like 'Senua dedende' (CD track 35) or a song with parts like 'All the earth is sacred' (CD track 33) or 'Shiwawa' (CD track 37).
9. Still want to carry on? Play 'What have you got already?' (section 1, activity 4) and when you have decided whether to play a part of your body or a piece of your surroundings you can enjoy even more of the activities in section 2, such as the 'Stop-start game', 'Rumbles', All about eight' etc.
10. End with a calming lullaby (section 5, activity 1) or if you've had enough singing for one day, make a 'Rainstorm'! (section 5, activity 4).

Resonance board half-hour session

Using the board on the floor

If you are using the board on the floor make sure the space is big enough for the board and for people to sit round the outside of it on the floor. Make things comfy for the players by putting mats or cushions around the outside of the board for people to sit on.

Start with everyone sitting round the outside and no one in the middle.

Activities

1. Begin by combining the 'Stop-start game' (section 2, activity 1) with 'Rumbles' (section 2, activity 2), using the board like a big drum.
2. Repeat this several times and then invite some people to put their feet or legs on the board to feel the vibration.
3. Then try 'Copy me do' (section 2, activity 10). Let all those who want to have a go at leading a rhythm.
4. Go back to number 1 but this time with someone lying on the board. Go gently, listen to the person on the board. (Read: 'What next?' for section 1, activity 6.)
5. Play the Pile up game (section 2, activity 14) using a rumble to pile up round the board and pile it down again.
6. Now repeat number 3, giving the person on the board a contrast between rumbles and organised beats.
7. Go on to play 'All about eight' (section 2, activity 8).
8. Finish with one of the lullabies (section 5, activity 2 & CD tracks 47, 48, 49 and 50).

Note: In a half hour session you will probably only have time to give 2 or 3 people a go on the board. Don't rush it, more people can have a go next time.

An evening in a youth club

A suggested programme of activities for working with a group of older children in a youth club setting

Activities

1. Begin by 'finding' instruments, using the ideas in 'What have you got already?' (section 1, activity 4).
2. Play simple rhythms on your 'instruments' – use 'Foodies' (section 2, activity 6) to get the ideas rolling.
3. Explain the idea of the basic beat and use either of the activities described in section 2, activity 3 to get a feel for it.
4. Combine the previous two activities and create a 'Pile up' (Section 2, activity 13).
5. Take it further with 'Orchestration' or if people are feeling really confident try 'Walking on the wall'.

Break

6. Gather together again and see if you can write some 'Instant songs' (section 3, activity 5).
7. Then combine your rhythm-making with your song-writing skills and see if you can 'Write a rap'. It can be good to work in small groups for this and then regroup to hear each others' raps.
8. That might be a great finale, but if they want more, why not try creating a 'Beginners' opera' (section 4, activity 3).
9. End on a natural high with the chant 'Zuma' (section 5, activity 1) or have some mutual appreciation with the Applaudion chair (section 5, activity 3).

A music theme day on a play-scheme

Preparation

Gather together scrap and materials for instrument making – cardboard tubes, containers, card, yoghurt pots, balloons, fillings for shakers etc (see activities in section 1 for more detail). You might like to make some sample instruments beforehand so children have something to copy or inspire them.

Depending on the size and venue of your playscheme, you are likely to have a range of activities on offer. We envisage a programme running throughout the day, alongside other play opportunities, with the potential for a whole group finale at the end of the day.

Morning session

Instrument making : Set up a workshop space with materials to make drums, shakers, wind instruments and even air guitars (section 1, activities 1, 2, 3 and 5). Children can spend as much or as little time as they want in making and decorating their creations. Once an instrument is finished get them to put their names on it, and tell them you will be playing some music games with them before lunchtime.

About half an hour before lunch gather together everyone who wants to play their instruments in a band and play some activities from section 2.

Activities

1. Play 'The Stop-start game' (section 2, activity 1) and get all those instruments heard.
2. Do some 'Rumbles' (section 2, activity 2).
3. Play 'One two who are you' (section 2, activity 4), using the instruments to play the 1, 2 beat.
4. Try 'After eight' (part of activity 8).
5. Finish with a chant like 'Jabulani' and get those instruments playing along to it.

Afternoon session

More games – Build on the morning session and take your rhythms a bit further. Try 'What's your name?' or 'Foodies'. See if you can organise a 'Pile up', and then have a go at 'Orchestration'.

Time for a story? Play 'Sound effects'. Use your instruments in a completely different way.

Half an hour before the end of the day why not gather everyone together for Musical cascade (section 4, activity 5)? Your 'musicians' can share the fun and show off their skills to the other children on the playscheme with this mini show where everyone gets to join in.

End the day with Applaudion chair so that everyone feels appreciated for the effort they have made – include instrument makers, instrument players, story-tellers, performers and audience.

Appendix 2

Words for Chants and Songs

We have learned these chants and songs in the African aural tradition over many years. We have written the words as we would say them and therefore want to apologise for any strangely spelled and incorrect words which may as a result change the original meaning of the chant. Where we know the meaning of the chant we have written this down.

Section 2 Finding a Rhythm

The Basic Beat Rap

CD track 3

Right & left & right & left
Feel it in your feet
It's the basic beat
mm- aah- mm mm- ah
Right & left & right & left
Fingers tap it in the car
Feet stamp it at the bar
It's the basic beat, feel it in your feet
mm- aah- mm mm- ah
Without this beat, music there is not
It's just sound and noise – so give it all you've got
Right & left & right & left
Feel it in your feet
It's the basic beat
mm- aah- mm mm- ah

Beat, Beat, Beat Upon the Tom-Tom!

CD track 14

Beat, beat, beat upon the Tom-Tom
Beat, beat, beat upon the Drum
Beat, beat, beat upon the Tom-Tom
Beat, beat, beat upon the Drum

Shuffle to the left, shuffle to the left
Shuffle shuffle shuffle shuffle, shuffle to the left
Shuffle to the right, shuffle to the right
Shuffle shuffle shuffle shuffle, shuffle to the right
AND
Beat, beat, beat upon the Tom-Tom
Beat, beat, beat upon the Drum
Beat, beat, beat upon the Tom-Tom
Beat, beat, beat upon the Drum

Section 3 Activity 6 Calls and chants

Jabulani

CD track 24

(Chant from South Africa - jubilation)

Jabulani jabulani ....
Jabulani jabulani ....
....
....
Jabulani jabulani ....

Listen to the CD track 24 to hear what you can put in the spaces.

Here are a few of our ideas but you can put anything you like in the spaces

Jabulani jabulani Africa
Jabulani jabulani Africa
Africa is hot and dry
Africa is hot and dry
Jabulani jabulani Africa

Jabulani jabulani singing songs
Jabulani jabulani singing songs
Makes you feel good, makes you happy
Makes you feel good, makes you happy
Jabulani jabulani singing songs

Jabulani jabulani Isabel
Jabulani jabulani Isabel
Lives in Swansea, comes from Zimbabwe
Lives in Swansea, comes from Zimbabwe
Jabulani jabulani Isabel

Hi Ya Ma

CD track 25

Hi ya ma, ga ga ma …………
Hi ha ma, ga ga ma oooh!
Hi ya ma, ga ga ma …………..
1 2 3 4

Listen to the CD track 25 to hear what you can put in the spaces.

Here is one idea using people's names

Hi ya ma, ga ga ma <u>Dai</u>
(everyone says the name of a person in the group)
Hi ha ma, ga ga ma <u>ooh!</u>
(everyone welcomes the person by saying ooh! - thumbs up)
Hi ha ma, ga ga ma <u>yeah!</u>
(person called has a space to reply with whatever they want, voice or percussion or action)
1 2 3 4

Helele Mama

CD track 26

Hey hey……………………..
Helele mama, helele mama
Hey hey……………………..
Helele mama, helele mama
Hey hey……………………..
Helele mama, helele ma-ma
Helele helele helele helele mama
Hey!

Listen to the CD track 26 to hear what you can put in the spaces.

Here is an idea using countries people are from. You can put whatever you like in the spaces.

Hey hey <u>Cymru</u>
Helele mama, helele mama
Hey hey <u>New Zealand</u>
Helele mama, helele mama
Hey hey <u>England</u>
Helele mama, helele ma-ma
Helele helele helele helele mama
Hey!

Here's another idea

Hey hey <u>cornflakes</u>
Helele mama, helele mama
Hey hey <u>rice krispies</u>
Helele mama, helele mama
Hey hey <u>muesli</u>
Helele mama, helele ma-ma
Helele helele helele helele <u>breakfast</u>
Hey

Ungawa

CD track 27

(This is a Native American welcome chant)

CALL	RESPONSE
Ungawa	
	Ungawa
Ungawa	
	Ungawa
Unga unga ungawa	
	Unga unga ungawa
Hey hey hey hey hey ungawa	
	Hey hey hey hey hey ungawa
Hey hey hey hey hey ungawa	
	Hey hey hey hey hey ungawa
Hey hey hey hey hey ungawa	
	Hey hey hey hey hey ungawa
Ungawa	
	Ungawa
Ungawa	
	Ungawa

Zumama

CD track 28

CALL	RESPONSE
Zu ma ma zum	
	Zum ma ma zum
Zu ma ma zum	
	Zum ma ma zum
Zouga – lou zouga-lou	
	Way – a!
Zouga – lou zouga-lou	
	Way – a!

Kpan Logo

CD track 29

(From Ghana - this is the name of a tribe, drum, dance and song used to celebrate puberty. The 'k' is silent)

CALL	RESPONSE
E- a - way	
	E - a - way
E-a - way	
	E- a - way
E Way-ay o ya	
	O- ya
E Way-ay o ya	
	O- ya
Mi-ni ma na ma no la	
	A lay lo
Mi-ni ma na ma no la	
	A lay lo
Kpan lo – go	
	Kpan lo –go
Kpan lo – go	
	Kpan lo -go
Kpan lo – go	
	Kpan lo -go
Kpan lo – go	
	Kpan lo -go

Wenn Oo Ma

CD track 30

Wenn oo ma jiggolo oh
Wenn oo ma jiggolo oh
Wenn oo ma jiggolo oh
Wenn oo ma jiggolo oh

Jii..........ga *(bang on drum)*
Wenn oo ma jigga *(bang on drum)*
Jii..........ga *(bang on drum)*
Wenn oo ma jigga OH

Tongoya

CD track 31

Na na na na na na na
Na na na na na na na na na na na na
Na na na na na na na
Na na na na na na na na na na na na

Na na na na.........
Na na na na.........
Na na na na.........
Na na na na.........
(Repeat)

Listen to the CD track 31 to hear what you can put in the spaces.

We used sounds, animal noises and fruits.

Na na na na Hey!
Na na na na Whoa!
Na na na na Ooh!
Na na na na Wheeee!
(Repeat)

Animal Noises - moo, baa, woof woof, meow
Fruit - banana, mango, kiwi, grapes

Aweninakile

CD track 32

A we-ni - na - ki - le
Mo ba-ko ne - wa fye
Oh Yeh, yeh, mo ba-ko ne - wa fye
Mo ba-ko ne - wa fye
Mo ba-ko ne - wa fye
Mo ba-ko ne - wa fye
Mo ba-ko ne - wa fye
Oh Yeh, yeh, mo ba-ko ne - wa fye
Yeh, yeh, mo ba-ko ne - wa fye

All the Earth is Sacred

CD track 33

All the Earth is sacred, ev'ry step we take
All the Earth is sacred, ev'ry step we take

Unite the people, we are one
Untie the people, we are one

All the air is sacred, ev'ry breath we take
All the air is sacred, ev'ry breath we take

Unite the people, we are one
Untie the people, we are one

The Earth is Our Mother

CD track 34

The Earth is our mother
We will take care of her
The Earth is our mother
We will take care of her

Hey yunga, ho yunga hey yung yung
Hey yunga ho yunga hey yung yung

Senua Dedende

CD track 35

Senua dedende senua
Senua dedende senua
Senua dedende senua dedende
Senua dedende senua

Kilele

CD track 36

(A walking song from Ghana - all 3 layers have the same words)

Kilele kilele oowa oowa kilele

Shiwawa

CD track 37

Two bottom layers:
Shiwawa shiwawa shiwawa shiwawa
(keep repeating)

Two top layers:
La shoni langu ma - ma ka – boo - yi
La shoni langu ma - ma ka – boo - yi
Si po - oo ma - ma ka – boo - yi
Si po – oo ma ma ka – boo yi

Toombady

CD track 38

(This is a Brazilian song - toombady means drum)

Layer 1:
Eh toombady, eh toombady, eh tapadoom, eh tapadoom, HUH

Layer 2 3 & 4:
Douwe toomba douwe ….. Shala la la

Layer 5:
Eh toombady, eh toombady, eh toombady eh eh

Section 3 Activity 7 Write a rap

The Body Rap

CD track 40

(This rap was written by Bobbie Stormont for a group of learning disabled young people)

Where is my head?
Why it's up here
Where are my feet?
Oh they are down there
I also have shoulders, elbows and wrists
And two hips for doing the twist
Then I have knees, ankles and heels
This is my body, how good it feels
Bottom, back, stomach, chest
Which part of my body do I like best?

CALL	RESPONSE
I like my hair	
	She likes her hair
I like my shoulders	
	She likes her shoulders
I like my eyes	
	She likes her eyes
I like my feet	
	He likes his feet
I like my toes	
	She likes her toes

This is my body , I like it....
YEAH!

Section 5 Activity 1 Zuma chant

Zuma

CD track 46

Layer 1:
Zuma - Zuma - Zuma - Zuma hey!

Layer 2:
Zuma hey Zuma - Zuma ho Zuma -

Layer 3:
This is exactly the same as layer 2 only it begins one beat after layer 3 (listen to the CD)
Zuma hey Zuma - Zuma ho Zuma -

Layer 4:
Zuma labba Zuma labba Zuma labba hey! hey!

Layer 5:
Africa hey hey hey hey-ey Zuma laba -

Layer 6:
Africa - a Zuma laba -

Section 5 Activity 2 Lullabies

Lullaby

CD track 47

La la la la la la
La la la la la la
La-a-la

Souallé

CD track 48

(Traditional African lullaby)

All 3 parts have just this one word

Soullaé soullaé soullaé soullaé
Soullaé soullaé soullaé soullaé
Soullaé soullaé soullaé soullaé
Soullaé soullaé soullaé soullaé

Bo Da Ya Da

CD track 49

CALL	RESPONSE
Mmmm bo da ya da	
	Mmmm bo da ya da
Mmmm bo da ya da	
	Mmmm bo da ya da
Mmmm bo da ya da	
	Mmmm bo da ya da
Mmmm bo da ya da	
	Mmmm bo da ya da

The Hawk

CD track 50

(South African Lullaby)

Sa ssu kro-ma
Ni-ne wa-na che che ko ko ma
Sa ssu kro-ma
Ni-ne wa-na che che ko ko ma
Sa ssu kro-ma
Ni-ne wa - a ko ko ma
Sa ssu kro-ma
Ni-ne wu - u ko ko ma

Bibliography, Sources and Useful Addresses

Books

Brewer, Chris and Campbell, Don G.: *Rhythms of Learning*. Zephyr Press 1991

Cookson, Paul (ed.): *The Works*. Poems chosen by Paul Cookson. Macmillan children's books 2000. Some great raps and especially how to write a rap.

Corke, M.: *Approaches to Communication through Music*. David Fulton Publishers 2002

Danes, Emma: *The Usborne First Book of Music*. Usborne Publishing Ltd. 1993

Davies, Alicia with William Gzowski: *Djembe Fundamentals*. Djembe techniques. Soar Valley Music, 1995

Diallo, Y. and Hall, M: *The Healing Drum*. Destiny Books 1989

'Drum Call' Magazine – free from www.drumcall.co.uk

Kershaw, Baz; and Coult, Tony: *Engineers of the Imagination*. Methuen 1983, revised 1990 (see www.welfare-state.org). Good for giant puppets and parades.

Pound, Linda and Harrison, Chris: *Supporting Musical Development in the Early Years*. Open University Press 2003

Leicestershire County Council Service: *Music*. Music for Children with Learning Difficulties. 1992

Marks, K. (ed.): *Circle of Song*. Songs chants and dances for ritual and celebration. Full Circle Press, revised 1995. P.O. box 428 Amherst M.A. 01004

Nichols, S.: *Bobby Shaftoe Clap Your Hands*. Musical fun with new songs from old favourites. A & C Black 1992

Orlick, Terry: *The Co-operative Sports and Games Book*. Writers and Readers Publishing Co-operative 1979 – reprinted 1982

Sanderson, A.(ed.): *Me*. Songs for 4-7 year olds. Ana Sanderson, A&C Black, 1997

Storms, G: *Handbook of Musical Games*, Hutchinson & Co, reprinted 1983

The Woodcraft Folk: *Games Games Games*. A co-operative games book. 3rd edition 1998

Umansky, K.: *Three Tapping Teddies*. Musical stories and chants for the very young. A & C Black (2000)

Umansky, K.: *Three Rapping Rats*. Making Music with traditional stories. A & C Black, 1998

Packs

TacPac – Tactile Approach to Communication. A pack consisting of tactile experiences set to music. Good for developing communication skills and sensory experiences for children with complex needs. Available from:'TacPac', Newdigate, Church Hill, Harefield, Middlesex UB9 6DX www.tacpac.co.uk

CDs

'Beat That!' – a selection of simple chants and rhythms that are easy to learn and play around with. They also support some of the games in 'Jabulani.'
Available from: Bobbie Stormont, Rose Cottage, Pound Lane, Stanton St John, OXON OX33 1HF

'Beats Working' CD – 'Traditional rhythms from 10 West African dances. Tracks 1-40 designed to assist learning, tracks 41-50 performed as they might be heard in the countries of origin.'
Available from: Beats Working, 59 Fernie Avenue, Melton Mowbray, Leicestershire LE13 0HZ

'Air Guitar 1' (2, 3 etc) – a series of CDs available from record shops. They contain classic tracks to play your air guitar along to!

Contacts for buying instruments

Goodies from Gambia
www.goodiesfromthegambia.co.uk

Soar Valley Music, Loughborough, (01509) 269629 (a place to get drums – good source and good value)

Search the internet for new suppliers

Interesting websites

www.bashthetrash.com (ideas for instrument making)

www.bbc.co.uk/radio3/world/onyourstreet/chlullaby1.shtm (listen to lullabies from around the world)

Other useful contacts

www.seriousfun.demon.co.uk (contact for Dynamix Ltd) Books available directly from Dynamix – *Serious Fun – Games for 4-9s* and *Serious Fun – Games for 10-14s*. Dynamix 2002

www.puppetsbypost.com (lovely puppets to buy)

www.stomp.co.uk

www.gis.net/~puppetco/ (The Puppeteer's Cooperative – great website for information on making puppets – especially giant ones)

For information and tour dates for Black Umfolosi – Zimbabwe's greatest ambassadors, performing traditional song and dance from Southern Africa – go to www.adastra-music.co.uk and follow the link to Black Umfolosi.

About the Authors

Carol Shephard has worked as a play worker, trainer and workshop facilitator since 1991 and has used music in all of these settings.

She has worked for the organisations 'Interplay' and 'Play Right' as a playleader and specialist playworker, running activities for groups of children, including children labelled 'special needs'. She has consistently brought music into these sessions through singing and playing on self-made instruments; on parades, on buses and anywhere else the children wanted to!

For the training co-operative Dynamix Limited, of which she is a director, she has run many training sessions for play- and youthworkers on using music with groups of children and young people. In facilitating conferences and consultations she has used music and song writing to encourage self-expression and to bring groups together. In 2001/2 she was co-author of the Dynamix publication *Participation – Spice It Up!* and also contributed to the two books of co-operative games called *Serious Fun: Games for 4 – 9s* and *Serious Fun: Games for 10 – 14s.*

Carol has played guitar since she was 5 years old, she is a competent drummer and she has sung in a 5-piece a-capella band for the past 9 years.

Bobbie Stormont has worked as a teacher since 1975, and trainer and workshop facilitator since 1993. Her teaching has included work with children, young people and adults with severe and complex learning needs where she has used movement and music as a foundation for many of their learning experiences. From this work her own approach to music teaching and music making has developed from 'playing it safe' – relying significantly on being able to read music and play guitar – to 'playing around': experimenting with sound, movement, chants and rhythms, improvising and making music more spontaneously so everyone can join in.

Within this area of work she was co-author of TACPAC, an activity pack bringing together music and tactile experiences to help develop communication skills.

As co-founder of 'Beat That!' – a training partnership – she has run many training sessions in play, education and business, using simple and effective techniques in live music-making to promote listening and communication skills and empower people to make and lead music. 'Beat That!' produced a CD of chants and drumming rhythms to support their training and workshops.

At conferences she has used music to energise groups, evaluate sessions, and bring events to a powerful and memorable end.

Bobbie learned music from an early age, playing piano and guitar and singing in choirs. She later furthered her training in singing and currently performs with a group called 'Friends in Concert'. Over the last 10 years she has learned to play djembe drum and uses drumming, percussion, singing and chanting in all her training and workshops.

Notes on CD

The CD has been recorded in both a studio and workshop setting. We recorded some tracks in the studio for clarity. The rest was recorded in a workshop because we wanted you to hear the games and chants as they sound when they are played in a more informal setting. As a result you may hear the odd car and truck go past and other sounds and imperfections that prove that it was a live recording.

Our workshop volunteers were not a group of professional musicians but a mixture of play workers, youth workers and friends. Most of them had never played these games before, nor were they very confident singers.

So our thanks go to Phill Burton, Pete Duncan, Dai Power, Bethan Morgan, Eddy Barnes, Beverley Haythor, Sue Maw, Katie Greenaway, Kelly Wake, Avril Harwood and Isabel Takawira – with a special thanks to Willis the sound engineer for performing both sides of the microphone.

Each track is introduced by the activity number it relates to and the title. At the beginning of each new section we tell you the number of that section too, just to reassure you where you are in relation to the book! The chants just have a title. Most tracks have a four beat introduction on wood blocks so you know when the track will start.

Those chants that have more than one part have been recorded so you hear the full chant with all its parts first and then you hear the individual parts that make up the chant. Don't be in any rush to learn and teach all the parts, take your time and feel really comfortable with the main part first. You will hear the chants sung through a few times only on the CD but when you are singing them with a group sing the main part over many times. You will experience how singing chants empowers and brings a group together. Once you are confident with the other main part then go on to teach the other parts one by one.

CD Track Listing

Section 2 - Finding a Rhythm

1. The stop-start game and rumbles (activities 1 and 2)
2. The basic beat – Legging it (activity 3)
3. The basic beat – The Body Rap (activity 3)
4. The basic beat – What next (activity 3)
5. One, two, who are you? (activity 4)
6. Vanessa's game (activity 5 – to a 4 beat marching rhythm)
7. Vanessa's game (activity 5 – to a 3 beat swing rhythm)
8. Foodies (activity 6)
9. What's your name? (activity 7)
10. What's your name? (activity 7 – different rhythm patterns with the same names)
11. All about eight (activity 8)
12. Number one to number five (activity 9)
13. Copy me do (activity 10)
14. Beat, beat, beat upon the tom-tom! (activity 11)
15. Pile up (activity 14)
16. Umfolosi Ulu (section 5 activity 3 – see drum roll on giving applause)

Section 3 - Finding your Voice

17. Warm up your body (activity 1)
18. Warm up your voice (activity 2)
19. Repeat after me (activity 3)
20. Vi vo vista (activity 3)
21. Sound bath (activity 4)
22. Instant songs (activity 5 – We like pizza and The Sound of Circus)
23. Calls and Chants (activity 6)

Calls and Chants (activity 6 and Appendix 2)

24. Jabulani
25. Hi ya Ma
26. Helele Mama
27. Ungawa
28. Zumama
29. Kpan Logo
30. Wenn oo ma
31. Tongoya
32. Awenimakile
33. All the Earth is Sacred
34. The Earth is Our Mother
35. Senua Dedende
36. Kilele
37. Shiwawa
38. Toombady

39. Write a rap (activity 7 – Smokin')
40. Write a rap (activity 7 – The Body Rap)
41. Let's improvise! (activity 8)

Section 4 - Finding Ways to Bring Music into Other Activities

42. Supporters' club (activity 2)
43. Beginners' opera (activity 3)
44. Music on the move (activity 6 – Samba)
45. Music on the move (activity 6 – Eight Train)

Section 5 - Finding an End

46. Zuma chant (activity 1)
47. Lullabies (described in activity 2)
48. Souallé (a lullaby)
49. Bo da ya da (a lullaby)
50. The Hawk (a lullaby)
51. Rainstorm (activity 4)

Other books from Hawthorn Press

The Singing Day

Songbook and CD for singing with young children

Candy Verney

Singing with babies is one of the joys of being a parent. It is a lifetime gift from you that children love. This easy to use songbook and CD offer practical help for singing with young children from birth to 4 years old.

'Opens our eyes to all the opportunities for singing that arise in a child's day, giving encouragement as well as practical tips.'

Caroline White, Stream of Sound Choir

160pp; 250 x 200mm; 1 903458 25 0; pb/CD

The Birthday Book

Celebrations for everyone

Ann Druitt, Christine Fynes-Clinton and Marije Rowling

Everything you need for celebrating birthdays in enjoyable ways. There are suggestions for 'oldies', for teenagers, 18th and 21st parties as well as children's parties. You will find unusual celebrations for those on holiday, ill in bed, at Christmas or for rainy days.

256pp; 250 x 200mm; paperback; 1 903458 01 3

All Year Round

Christian calendar of celebrations

Ann Druitt, Christine Fynes-Clinton, Marije Rowling

All Year Round is brimming with things to make; activities, stories, poems and songs to share with your family. It is full of well-illustrated ideas for fun and celebration: from Candlemas to Christmas and Midsummer's day to the Winter solstice.

Observing the round of festivals is an enjoyable way to bring rhythm into children's lives and provide a series of meaningful landmarks to look forward to. Each festival has a special character of its own: participation can deepen our understanding and love of nature and bring a gift to the whole family.

320pp; 250 x 200mm; paperback; 1 869 890 47 7

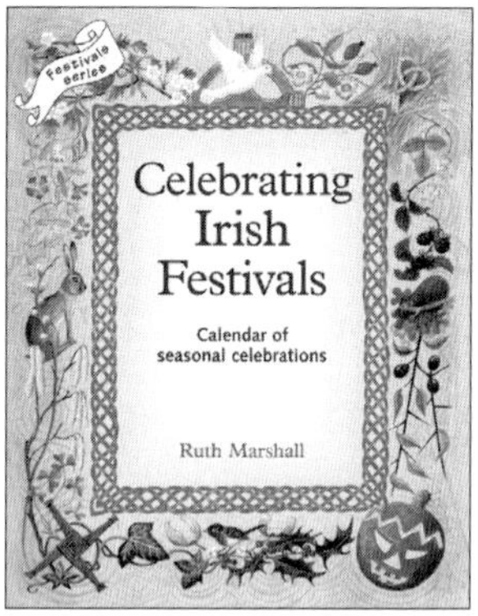

Celebrating Irish Festivals

Calendar of seasonal celebrations

Ruth Marshall

If you are interested in Irish traditions, need a family or school resource, then here is an inspiring treasury of stories, beautiful illustrations, poems, traditions, food, activities, games, dances and songs. Reaching back to the ancient festivals of Imbolc, Bealtaine, Lughnasadh, Samhain, and to Celtic Christianity – Ruth Marshall also offers new ways for engaging children.

'A comprehensive calendar of festivals that children will cherish.'

Ireland's Own, Summer 2003

224pp; 250 x 200mm; paperback; 1 903458 23 4

The Children's Year

Seasonal crafts and clothes

Stephanie Cooper, Christine Fynes-Clinton, Marije Rowling

You needn't be an experienced craftsperson to create beautiful things! This step by step, well-illustrated book with clear instructions shows you how to get started. Children and parents are encouraged to try all sorts of handwork, with different projects relating to the seasons of the year.

Here are soft toys, wooden toys, moving toys, such as balancing birds or climbing gnomes, horses, woolly hats, mobiles and dolls. Designs and patterns for children's clothing are included, using natural fabrics. Over 100 treasures to make, in seasonal groupings.

192pp; 250 x 200mm; paperback; 1 869 890 00 0

Festivals, Family and Food

Guide to seasonal celebration

Diana Carey and Judy Large

This family favourite is a unique, well-loved source of stories, recipes, things to make, activities, poems, songs and festivals. Each festival such as Christmas, Candlemas and Martinmas has its own, well-illustrated chapter.

There are also sections on Birthdays, Rainy Days, Convalescence and a birthday Calendar. The perfect present for a family, it explores the numerous festivals that children love celebrating.

224pp; 250 x 200mm
paperback; 0 950 706 23 X

'It's an invaluable resource book' *The Observer*
'Every family should have one' *Daily Mail*

Festivals Together

Guide to multicultural celebration

Sue Fitzjohn, Minda Weston, Judy Large

This special book for families and teachers helps you celebrate festivals from cultures from all over the world. This resource guide for celebration introduces a selection of 26 Buddhist, Christian, Hindu, Jewish, Muslim and Sikh festivals. It offers a lively introduction to the wealth of different ways of life. There are stories, things to make, recipes, songs, customs and activities for each festival, comprehensively illustrated.

You will be able to share in the adventures of Anancy the spider trickster, how Ganesh got his elephant head and Eid, Holi, Wesak, Advent, Divali, Chinese New Year and more.

224pp; 250 x 200mm paperback; 1 869 890 46 9

'The ideal book for anyone who wants to tackle multicultural festivals.'
Nursery World

Games Children Play

How games and sport help children develop

Kim John Payne

Illustrated by Marije Rowling

Games Children Play offers an accessible guide to games with children of age three upwards. These games are all tried and tested, and are the basis for the author's extensive teacher training work.

The book explores children's personal development and how this is expressed in movement, play, songs and games. Each game is clearly and simply described, with diagrams or drawings, and accompanied by an explanation of why this game is helpful at a particular age. The equipment that may be needed is basic, cheap and easily available.

192pp; 297 x 210mm; paperback; 1 869 890 78 7

The Islamic Year

Surahs, Stories and Celebrations

Noorah Al-Gailani and Chris Smith

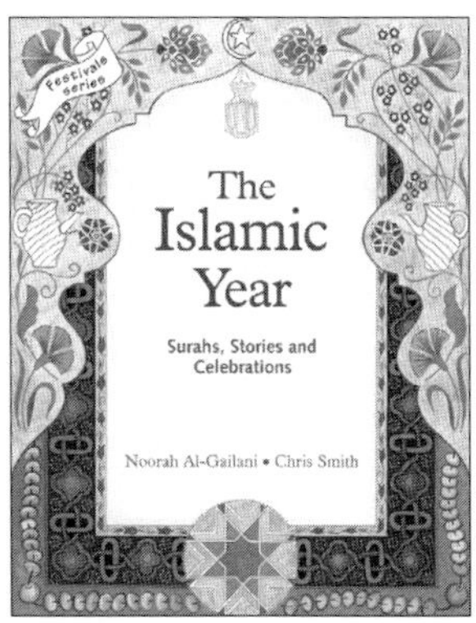

Celebrate the Islamic Year in your family or at school! You are invited to explore Muslim festivals with this inspiring treasury of stories, surahs, songs, games, recipes, craft and art activities. Folk tales illustrate the core values of Islamic culture with gentle humour and wisdom. *The Islamic Year* is beautifully illustrated with traditional patterns, maps and pictures drawn from many parts of the Muslim world, and Arabic calligraphy.

240pp; 250 x 200mm; paperback; 1 903458 14 5

Pull the Other One!

String Games and Stories Book 1

Michael Taylor

This well-travelled and entertaining series of tales is accompanied by clear instructions and explanatory diagrams – guaranteed not to tie you in knots and will teach you tricks with which to dazzle your friends!
'A practical and entertaining guide, which pulls together a wealth of ideas from different cultures and revives a forgotten art.... Sheila Munro, parenting author

128pp; 216 x 148mm; drawings; paperback; 1 869 890 49 3

Now You See It...

String Games and Stories Book 2

Michael Taylor

String Games are fun, inviting children to exercise skill, imagination and team-work. They give hands and fingers something clever and artistic to do! Following the success of *Pull the Other One!*, here are more of Michael Taylor's favourite string games, ideal for family travel, for creative play and for party tricks.

136pp; 216 x 148mm; paperback; 1 903458 21 8

Ordering books

If you have difficulties ordering Hawthorn Press books from a bookshop, you can order direct from: **Booksource,** 32 Finlas Street, Glasgow G22 5DU
Tel: (08702) 402182 Fax: (0141) 557 0189 E-mail: orders@booksource.net

or you can order online at **www.hawthornpress.com**

For further information or a book catalogue, please contact:

Hawthorn Press, 1 Lansdown Lane, Stroud, Gloucestershire GL5 1BJ
Tel: (01453) 757040 Fax: (01453) 751138 E-mail: info@hawthornpress.com
Website: www.hawthornpress.com

Dear Reader

If you wish to follow up your reading of this book, please tick the boxes below as appropriate, fill in your name and address and return to Hawthorn Press:

☐ Please send me a catalogue of other Hawthorn Press books.

☐ Please send me details of Education events and courses.

Questions I have about Education are:

Name ______________________________

Address ______________________________

____

Postcode ______________ Tel. no. ______________

Please return to:

Hawthorn Press, 1 Lansdown Lane, Stroud, Gloucestershire. GL5 1BJ, UK
or Fax (01453) 751138

JAB